Walk With God

A Simple Man's Journey to
Meaningful Prayer,
Deeper Faith and
Experiencing Miracles

By Rick Rupp

Walk With God: A Simple Man's Journey to Meaningful Prayer, Deeper Faith and Experiencing Miracles by Rick Rupp

Scripture quotations are taken from the Holy Bible, New King James Version (R), Copyright 1982 by HarperCollins (a subsidary of **News Corp**). All rights reserved.

Cover design by Jennifer Lassiter.

Table of Contents

Endorsements

Wow! *Walk With God* is an incredible read which will strengthen your faith, your prayer life and encourage you greatly. A must read!

~ Jim Lange, Founder of 5feet20.com
and author of *Calming the Storm Within,
How to Find Peace in This Chaotic World*,
Toledo, Ohio.

I've been blessed to know Rick for almost 20 years. He impacted my life the first time praying for me. He impacted my life a second time watching God use him in the Solomon Islands. He impacted my life again while reading this book. I encourage you to take this journey with Rick and watch God impact your life.

~ Al Caperna, Chairman of CMC Group,
Bowling Green, Ohio.

I have known Rick Rupp since January 2001. Both of our lives were in a divine transition at the time and Rick invited me to live in his home for 5 months until I could move my family. He is the real man that he says he is! The journey of his life explained in this book is fascinating and will have the result of increasing your hunger for Christ. I am so happy that I get to be involved in his life!

~ Mike Shinkle, Pastor of Open Way Church, Topeka, Kansas.

I have known Rick for almost 40 years and can truly say his life is a desire for 'one thing'. It is no exaggeration to say the work that he is doing in the South Pacific islands is changing the nations, in both the natural and the spiritual. He is a man of determination and faithfulness in things little and big. I'm grateful to have been on the journey with him and know you will be challenged to reach for more of God's plan for your life after reading his story.

~ Steve Stutzman, Pastor of Open Way Church, Topeka, Kansas.

Walk With God is a remarkable story which outlines the spiritual and practical journey of a man sent to meet the needs of the people in remote villages of the Solomon Islands and Papua New Guinea for clean drinking water, medical assistance and the promise that 'To him who is thirsty I will give to drink without cost from the spring of the water of life.' (Revelation 21:6)

It is a riveting read!

~ Jenny Hagger, Director of Australian House of Prayer For All Nations, Adelaide, Australia.

Read this book! Twice I've traveled with Rick Rupp to the Solomon Islands. I watched the tractor well rig team install water wells. I tasted the water! I experienced the joy and excitement of these Island people who are too poor to purchase a water well but are blessed with a Clean Water 4 Life sponsored well. I've seen the good fruit from this ministry! This ministry is changing these nations and God is being glorified! Support this ministry!

~ Steve Brandt, President, Steve's Livestock Transport, Blumenort, Manitoba, Canada.

Foreword

Isaiah tells us that from the ends of the earth we will hear songs and the coastlands will sing glory to the Righteous One, who is the beautiful God-Man, Christ Jesus (Isaiah 42:10). Before the return of Jesus, God will establish a global prayer and worship movement and the gospel will be preached to every tribe, tongue and nation (Matthew 24:14). Even today, thousands of prayer rooms have been established all over the globe, many of those going day and night. In remote small jungle villages, such as Fa'arau, there is a 24/7 prayer room giving glory to Jesus continually, with or without electricity. This is a sign and a wonder pointing to the worth of Jesus and His soon return. Here at The International House of Prayer, Kansas City (IHOPKC), we long to see 24/7 prayers for justice combine with 24/7 acts of justice. Like the woman Anna in Luke 2, she spent long hours engaged in prayer and fasting. This 84 year-old woman gave over 60 years of her life to this lifestyle. She was able to see the answer to prayer for the Messiah when she saw Jesus as a baby with her own eyes. This launched her not only into a lifestyle of prayer and fasting in the temple, but also into doing justice and the work of the kingdom by telling many that Jesus is the Messiah. Anna is an example we set before ourselves as intercessory missionaries—this is a calling for men and women, both old and young.

Rick Rupp is one of those such men, like Anna, who has given his life to prayer and fasting and doing the work of the kingdom. Rick Rupp joined IHOPKC in 2001, when our prayer room was just beginning and still in the little trailers. His life is a strong testimony of how God uses night and day prayer to bring healing to wounded hearts. The first few years at IHOPKC, Rick spent long hours in the prayer room as the woman Anna in Luke 2. During this time, he served as a prayer leader and usher. In 2004 Rick joined our nightwatch, praying from midnight to 6am. He continued to prayer lead and he also offered healing prayer for many each night. Rick became affectionately known as the "nightwatch dad". I remember hearing Rick crying out for revival in Topeka, Kansas, praying for the church to unite and establish a 24/7 prayer room. Since 2001 he has driven to Topeka once a week giving leadership to the Topeka House of Prayer. As

Rick's faith grew and as God transformed his heart and life, God began to share His heart for the poor in the Solomon Islands and Papua New Guinea. After years of abandoning himself to prayer and fasting, Rick then began to launch into bringing justice to the poor of the earth in the name of Jesus and also calling the poor of the earth into the Anna calling. Rick is the "real thing"—he is a model for others to follow as he engages in long hours of prayer and combines this with works of justice. He has some amazing stories of this journey of pursuing a spirit of prayer and his journey to the islands which are written in the pages of this book.

Mike Bickle
Director, International House of Prayer of
Kansas City

Section 1

The Call

The Struggle To Have A Meaningful Prayer Life

Chapter 1
The Call

God used my season of crisis and pain to suddenly break into my life at the moment of my attempting to commit suicide. Yes, God thundered in an audible voice as I was a step or two away from electrocuting myself in our backyard swimming pool, thundering from heaven, *"Rick, STOP! Now you know how I feel. My bride has done the exact same thing and has run off with other lovers."*

At first I was stunned because I did not think that God still spoke to people in an audible voice. I did not understand that Jesus was a Bridegroom God with jealous emotions.

I was in utter agony and brokenness dealing with the pain and rejection of being dumped for another man after 24 years of marriage. I felt such a failure and utterly hopeless. So why not end the pain and proceed with my plan to end my life? Suddenly God thundered a second time from heaven saying *"Rick, STOP! Now you know how I feel. My bride has done the exact same thing and has run off with other lovers."* But this time He added, *"Rick, I am looking for a friend who will stand in the gap and make intercession. Will you join me?"*

God in His great mercy intervened and stopped my plan to electrocute myself in our swimming pool. After unplugging the electrical cord of the leaf blower machine I entered our kitchen and collapsed onto the linoleum floor and wept. I was overwhelmed that my Savior Jesus Christ, whom I knew and loved, would shout from heaven and rescue a wretch like me!

My Pastor had been mentoring and helping me through this 2-year marriage crisis from day one. I remember him sharing with me during the first of many counseling sessions how most men would use drugs, alcohol, or even porn to medicate their pain. I am so thankful that his advice to me at that critical moment was not to go down that road. He recommended that I should give myself, instead, to a lifestyle of prayer and fasting.

Prior to my suicide attempt, on that very same day I decided I would drive and tell my Pastor what I was planning to do. When we met I told him I had done everything he had asked me to do and it just did not work. I went on to explain that I had devised the perfect plan so my wife could have the life-insurance money, our home debt free, and she could be free from the guilt of living in adultery with another man and be free to marry her lover.

It was an intense moment with my Pastor, who had invested so much time and prayer, including a 40-day water fast, to see my marriage restored. Softly in a trembling voice and with tears in his eyes he told me that he would be praying that God would interrupt my suicide plan.

Sometime after the audible voice experience, I awoke several hours later on our kitchen floor. I was in a mess. Lying in a pool of snot with tears on the floor. All I could think about was sharing my experience with my Pastor. After all, he had said he would be praying that God would stop me.

So I decided I would get up off the floor and give him a call. I really hoped and expected that we could meet immediately. The first words out of his mouth were "Rick, you're alive! You didn't do it!" I smiled and said, "Pastor, I need to come over to your house immediately. I have something

5

powerful to share with you." Unfortunately, he said that his family had evening plans so instead he scheduled a lunch meeting with me the next day at Bennigans. Sadly, I said, "OK, but you aren't going to believe what just happened," and hung up.

That next day at lunch provided me an even greater depth of understanding of God's plan for my life. After explaining to my Pastor how God had intervened and saved my life, this is what he shared with me. First, he opened up his Bible to Ezekiel 22:30 and read it to me.

So I sought for a man among them who would make a wall, and stand in the gap before Me on behalf of the land, that I should not destroy it; but I found no one. (Ezekiel 22:30)

Frankly I was surprised that God had spoken a very similar word to Ezekiel. I had never heard of, nor read, this Bible verse. Since God had spoken to me saying, *"Rick, I am looking for a friend who will stand in the gap and make intercession. Will you join Me?"* I asked my Pastor what this meant.

He shared that I should pray about quitting my job and moving to Kansas City to join the International House of Prayer. Reluctantly I responded that our small Open Way Church would suffer financially without my tithe. Then, with energy that I'd rarely seen from my Pastor and friend he looked at me and said, "Rick Rupp, we do not need a man who makes a lot of money. We need a man with the spirit of prayer on his life!"

Now I was trembling because this was new information that was baffling to me. For the next few minutes I sat and listened to every word that flowed from my Pastor's lips.

He shared how, when my wife announced she was leaving me for another man, he had gone on a 40-day water fast on behalf of my marriage. Plus, on a previous fast, he had cried out to God for a teenager addicted to drugs and that neither time of his prayer and fasting had produced deliverance or healing. He said, "As a Pastor I feel so impotent". He said, "Where is the power to heal broken marriages and where is the power to set the drug addicts free?"

He continued by saying that in 1998 he had attended the Passion for Jesus Conference hosted in Kansas City by Mike Bickle's Church. He had heard Mike Bickle say that part of the vision for day and night prayer was to contend for the restoration of an apostolic anointing on every congregation. My Pastor said the longing of his heart was for another great outpouring of the Holy Spirit with powerful signs and wonders as the norm, not the exception.

Of course, now I was beginning to get a grasp of my Pastor's desperation for revival because he was right. It was because there was little or no prayer, there was little or no power on the preaching of the Gospel. This was such a radical idea that I initially resisted it for several reasons. I could not imagine myself being effective in a prayer ministry. Every time previously that I had tried the prayer thing, it had proved to be a boring, short lived attempt. After 5 minutes on my knees I would always run out of things to pray.

My Pastor also counseled me saying that I should grant my wife an uncontested divorce. He actually came with me to the Court House on December 19, 2000 to pray for me and be there to support me during this most difficult day. The marriage was over with the stroke of the judge's signature granting the divorce. Several months later our home in Topeka was sold and with $5,000 in the bank I took my Pastor's advice, quit my job, and set off to join the International House of Prayer in Kansas City. I departed on May 17, 2001.

Chapter 2
The Struggle to Have a Meaningful Prayer Life

I'll never forget walking through the doors of the International House of Prayer in Kansas City on May 17, 2001. The IHOPKC staff had grown to approximately 200 people. Mike Bickle, the Director, announced that we were all jumping right into a 21-day corporate fast. Don't get me wrong, I was excited to be part of this prayer and fasting ministry but I was not sure if I could live 21 days without food.

I talked this 21-day fasting event over with my Topeka Pastor and together we decided that I would eat only watermelon for 21 days. That seemed like a good solution to a rookie prayer guy with little fasting experience on his resume. I decided I would read the Bible from cover to cover during this season. So initially I signed up for 12–

hour days in the prayer room, Monday – Saturday, 6am–6 pm. I confess that during the 21 day fast I still drank a Latte every morning, but the fast proved to be a very wise beginning to my journey into obtaining a "spirit of prayer".

The other thing I really liked during this initial 21-day fast was the afternoon time of teaching by Mike Bickle and the time he made for testimonies. Mike made room for people to share their God encounters such as dreams, visions or revelations. It was a real treat for me to listen to all this teaching on prayer and fasting. It was also obvious that I was doing this prayer thing with several hundred "hungry for God" people. It was really amazing for me to hear numerous people stand up and share publically about receiving a dream or a vision. I even received a dream, but I was not bold enough to stand up in front of people to share anything yet!

It had been decades since I had experienced any spiritual activity in my life, so this dream, including the spiritual understanding, was another stepping stone to reconnecting to Father's heart for me. In the dream, I saw a cluster of green grapes. Initially I thought the green grapes were ready to be picked and eaten, but to my surprise they were still green and hard, which showed me that they were young and would require time to mature. In my dream I asked God what He was speaking to me. I was slightly miffed and I said something like: "So, God are You telling me that I'm an immature believer or what?" God replied calmly in a Fatherly tone and said, "Rick look closer and tell Me what you see." I said, "I see a cluster of really healthy tiny grapes growing on a really healthy vine and there is no insect damage. They look spotless and in due time will be delicious." I calmed down and said, "Okay God, what exactly are You trying to share with me?" Then I understood His heart. God was saying "Rick the spiritual growth that you desire will take time to develop. There was no quick fix to my problems. I understood that there was no short cut in this journey.

I thought that it would take me around 6 months at the most to get a 'spirit of prayer' on my life, then I would be returning to Topeka, Kansas. But I discerned from this encounter that I would need to slow down and allow God all the time necessary to fully mature me into a fruitful prayer warrior.

So my journey started with a mandate from heaven to slow down and allow God all the time He needed to reshape my life.

In those early IHOPKC days my most common daily prayer was pretty simple. "Abba, please help me. I don't know how to pray. I don't know how or what it means to slow down and 'wait upon the Lord', and I don't hear Your voice very well." Unfortunately no one had ever taught me that there were lots of prayers in the Bible, except of course the Lord's Prayer which I did know, but that was it. Things were about to change drastically because now I was sitting under the teaching of Mike Bickle at IHOPKC.

It was a season of spending long hours reading and meditating on God's Word. Psalm 119 seemed to be jumping off the page and helping me understand that I was not alone in this quest for a deeper walk with God. Please look with me for a moment at the first portion of Psalm 119 and delight in God's Word:

1 *Blessed* are *the undefiled in the way,*
Who walk in the law of the Lord!

2 *Blessed* are *those who keep His testimonies,*
Who seek Him with the whole heart!

3 *They also do no iniquity;*
They walk in His ways.

4 *You have commanded us*
To keep Your precepts diligently.

5 *Oh, that my ways were directed*
To keep Your statutes!

6 *Then I would not be ashamed,*
When I look into all Your commandments.

7 *I will praise You with uprightness of heart,*
When I learn Your righteous judgments.

8 *I will keep Your statutes;*
Oh, do not forsake me utterly!

9 *How can a young man cleanse his way?*
By taking heed according to Your word.

10 *With my whole heart I have sought You;*
Oh, let me not wander from Your commandments!

11 *Your word I have hidden in my heart,*
That I might not sin against You.

It wasn't long before I became familiar with praying Biblical prayers. I was sitting 12 hours a day in a prayer room where people like Mike Bickle,

Allen Hood, and Misty Edwards were praying apostolic prayers on the microphone. I sure aspired to pray like they did.

They seemed to be in the process of learning how to flow with the worship team. While one person prayed a Biblical prayer on the microphone, the worship team of 3 or 4 singers would jump right into the person's prayer and sing phrases from the scripture being prayed. Then before long it somehow erupted into a catchy little chorus so us folks sitting in the room could actually get involved in the prayer by singing the chorus, repeating it over and over, until we would hear the lead singer give everyone a cue by singing, "O God". Apparently, that "O God" meant that the person praying on the microphone should pray some more. Soon the singers would jump right back into the prayer by singing short scriptural phrases, until once again it developed into a corporate chorus. This was nice because us people in the room could sing along with the singers. I really liked this new style of prayer! It was enjoyable!

I laugh now, looking back on the early days of my journey. I remember sitting down at one of the tables with my Bible and Mike Bickle's personal assistant would walk over, place a box of tissues next to my Bible, and whisper in my ear that she was glad to see the weeping prophet! It was awkward for me, because I was still hurting from the divorce. I was carrying so much guilt and shame that I couldn't talk to anyone about my failed marriage and I was trying to cope with the learning curve of prayer and fasting as a lifestyle. I had no income and the $5,000 I had in savings was dwindling down. Yet I knew that I knew that God had a plan for my life and that I needed to stick out this prayer assignment!

There was a war going on inside my heart. I was sitting in the prayer room and one day I heard the worship team singing, "The Lord is good and His mercy endures forever. The Lord is gracious and compassionate and He does not give us what our sins deserve." I thought to myself, "God, which is it? The devil is telling me that I'm disqualified and Your Word is saying that You are great in mercy? God, which is it? God, I have to know! How great is Your mercy?"

Over the next months, I can't tell you how many times I struggled with condemnation and the prophetic singers would never fail to start singing over me things like "Stand fast!" "Don't give up!" "The Lord is fighting for you!" "The truth will set you free!" I would sing with the prophetic singers songs like, "I'll hold fast and I'll stand firm."

During that season, I remember listening to a Mike Bickle sermon from Isaiah 61:7

Instead of your shame you shall have double honor, And instead of confusion they shall rejoice in their portion. Therefore in their land they shall possess double; Everlasting joy shall be theirs. (Isaiah 61:7)

I had to repent of a wrong view of God because I thought he was mad at me. After all, I had read in Malachi that God hates divorce so I improperly translated this to mean that He now hated me. I was beginning to see that I had totally underestimated the grace and mercy that God was offering to me. It was a combination of my reading and praying God's Word, the IHOPKC prophetic singers washing me with the truth of God's Word on a daily basis, and great Biblical teaching that began to bring inner healing to my hurting heart. I began asking God to restore my dignity and to give me the oil of joy for my mourning.

During this season of much inner healing and inner turmoil I felt the Holy Spirit inviting me into another 21 day fast, but the only person I told about this fast was my Pastor in Topeka. I had another profound encounter at the end of this fast that communicated once and for all that God is overwhelmingly in love with me and His mercy is so far beyond my comprehension.

This special God encounter happened in November of 2001 on the final day of my fast. I remember it was an unusually warm 65-degree day, sunny and beautiful outside. I was tempted to spend that afternoon in a park outside somewhere, but I am so glad I didn't do this.

I think there were maybe three of us in the prayer room that sunny afternoon when the encounter happened.

There was a full worship team singing and ministering to the Lord up front and I was prayer walking towards the back of the prayer room. I felt the finger of God inside my belly motioning and inviting me to deeper communion. When my eyes landed on the communion table at the other end of the prayer room I discerned that this was Jesus inviting me to take the communion elements. Then I thought, "Hey, I can't take communion twice in one day." I remembered taking the communion elements at 6am that morning. However the intensity of God's touch increased in my inner man, convincing me that this was God. So I walked over to take the elements.

I held the cracker and, like I had done hundreds of times over my years of being a Christian, I said, "Rick, take and eat. This is the body of Christ broken for you. Jesus, I eat this bread in remembrance of Your sacrifice for me on the cross." After eating the cracker, I took the grape juice and prayed, "Rick, take and drink. This is the new covenant of Jesus' blood shed for you for the remission of all of your sins. Jesus, I drink this in remembrance of Your great love and mercy for me. Thank You, Jesus!"

The moment that the grape juice touched my lips the heavens were opened and I was now looking up into eyes of Jesus Christ which were like flames of fire. Suddenly, lightning shot from His eyes down into my eyes resounding into a loud sonic BOOM in my inner man with His thunderous voice saying, "Rick, I like you! I forgive you! Get over it!"

I was so overcome at that moment that I looked over at the worship team expecting them to all be prostrate on the floor. It was such a terrifying moment, that I expected everyone present to be terrified also, but they were not a part of this encounter. They were singing and worshiping totally unaware of what had just happened to me at the communion table. I turned my glance back up, hoping to see His face, but Jesus was no longer there. It was now back to a white ceiling. I lifted my fist towards heaven and said, "Don't You ever do that again, because it was so terrifying!" I thought for a second and changed my request and said, "O dear God, please do that again!" Nothing like this has ever occurred again, but I go to the communion table with expectation, knowing it could happen again!

Beholding the face of Jesus led me to develop a new prayer. For thirty plus days after this electrifying experience, I was in a state of awe and all I could think and say was, "He likes me! I'm forgiven! I'm His favorite!" So here is the new prayer that has become a daily prayer ever since that special encounter. I whisper this prayer over and over throughout my day. I whisper this prayer whenever I enter a home, a business, a church, a Walmart, or anywhere I go. Here it is: *"Lord it's me again, Your favorite, the one You like, the one You enjoy seeing, asking that the God of our Lord Jesus Christ, the Father of Glory may give to us the Spirit of wisdom and revelation in the knowledge of Jesus Christ."*

Section 2

The Three Golden Nuggets

Chapter 3
Golden Nugget #1

The Apostle Paul gives us three golden nuggets in the Book of Ephesians. Golden Nugget number 1 is found in Ephesians 1.

16 I do not cease to give thanks for you, making mention of you in my prayers: 17 that the God of our Lord Jesus Christ, the Father of glory, may give to you the spirit of wisdom and revelation in the knowledge of Him, 18 the eyes of your understanding[a] being enlightened; that you may know what is the hope of His calling, what are the riches of the glory of His inheritance in the saints, 19 and what is the exceeding greatness of His power toward us who believe, according to the working of His mighty power 20 which He worked in Christ when He raised Him from the dead and seated Him at His right hand in the heavenly places.(Ephesians 1:16-20).

I cannot overemphasize the power of praying God's Word. And when I say praying the Bible, I also mean singing the prayers of the Bible, which I do daily. As my journey continued as a full-time intercessor at the Kansas City International House of Prayer, it became obvious that this prayer of the Apostle Paul in Ephesians 1:17-18 is by far the prayer that is most often prayed on the microphone. I even got bold enough to pray on the microphone and began praying this prayer for the Church in Topeka, Kansas.

I found it perplexing that I had been a Christian since April 20, 1973 and never heard this prayer prayed until that first week in May of 2001. In fact, during all those years of being in Church Sunday morning after Sunday morning I cannot ever recall hearing even one sermon about praying the prayers that are found throughout the Bible. Now I was immersed in a House of Prayer where Ephesians 1:17-18 was being prayed every day and every night. Some prayer meetings at IHOPKC included 8 people in a row praying this prayer over a city or a nation during one two-hour segment. It didn't take long before I had it memorized.

I discovered that most of the prayers recorded in the Bible were addressed as prayers for the Church in a city. Ephesians 1:1 says this prayer was written to be prayed for the Church that is in the city of Ephesus- the faithful Ephesians in Christ Jesus.

"Paul, an apostle of Jesus Christ by the will of God, to the saints who are in Ephesus, and faithful in Christ Jesus" (Ephesians 1:1).

It is interesting to note that Paul was giving us divine insight. This was a new life changing revelation that was finally beginning to make sense to me. If Paul primarily focused on praying positive prayers like Ephesians 1:17-18, then I wanted to learn this Biblical model. In my journey, I soon discovered a pattern in the Bible. I recommend you also take some time to study the scriptural prayers. In the appendix I will include a list of Biblical prayers. My prayer is for you to discover, like I did, that in the New Testament we mostly find the Church leaders praying for the Church to become the Church. Praying positive Biblical prayers is brilliant!

So, I have some really good news! This Ephesians 1:17-18 prayer works for anything you want to pray for. I pray this prayer for myself, my siblings, my Pastor, our President, my children, my grandchildren, the ending of abortion in our nation, for the ending of human trafficking, for lost family and friends, for Israel, for terrorists, and more.

Why does God want us to pray this Ephesians 1:17-18 prayer? Personally, I need a greater revelation of Jesus every day. I need to grow in the knowledge of God. I need my eyes to open to see Him rightly. I need to know the hope to which He has called me. I need to understand that I am His inheritance. I really need the exceeding greatness of His power to help me die to myself and become transformed into His image. Like my Pastor said, "Rick, we need a man with a spirit of prayer!"

My goal in writing this book is to share some of my personal experiences so perhaps my testimonies will encourage you to pursue the spirit of prayer as well!

One of my heroes in the Bible, who operated in a spirit of prayer, is mentioned in Colossians 4:12. It says:

"Epaphras, who is one of you, a bondservant of Christ, greets you, always laboring fervently for you in prayers, that you may stand perfect and complete in all the will of God" (Colossians 4:12).

I want this same Epaphras anointing! Paul says, that Epaphras is a servant of Christ. My goal is to be a servant of Christ! Wow am I ever provoked with those three words that Paul uses to describe this servant who prays that the Church may stand perfect and complete in all the will of God, **always laboring fervently**. That's my desire too!

What does Paul mean about brother Epaphras when he writes 'always laboring fervently'? When people ask my kids about how their Dad is doing I hope my life is such that they would say, "Oh, Dad's always laboring fervently!"

Colossians 4 has several other verses I want you to see. Colossians 4:2 says, *"Continue earnestly in prayer, being vigilant in it with thanksgiving"* and Colossians 4:13 says, *"For I bear him witness that he has a great zeal for you* (Colossians 4:13).

I want to walk in this same great zeal and be found faithful to continue in prayer with an anointing to always labor fervently for the Church, to stand perfect and complete in all the will of God with a thankful heart. I believe God is raising up others with this same passion for praying for the Church.

Would you agree that if every city in our nation had an expression of prayer like Epaphras, things would certainly be much better in our families, schools, and government?

Let me continue with one more thought on prayer. Philippians 4:6 says, *"Be anxious for nothing, but in everything by prayer and supplication, with thanksgiving, let your requests be made known to God."* It does not say, "But in a few things by prayer and supplication......let your requests be made known."

God has highlighted to me the power of praying 'with thanksgiving!' In my second year of serving at IHOPKC I became a prayer leader for one of the worship teams. I love prayer leading at IHOPKC. During our times of intercession we involve the people sitting in the chairs by inviting them to join the prayer leader by praying on the microphone. This is what we call 'rapid fire' prayer. On occasion I have invited people to pray and offer up rapid-fire prayers of thanksgiving. We invite each person to pray a quick 10-second prayer, giving thanks to God for something specific.

The fruit of praying prayers of thanksgiving is joy! Over the past 12 years that I have been a prayer leader at IHOPKC I've noticed repeatedly that offering up these rapid-fire prayers of thanksgiving releases great joy in the prayer room, changing the atmosphere! Everyone in the room is smiling and engaged as we thank God for the many things He has done in our lives!

In 2003 we were training musicians, singers, and prayer leaders from both Topeka and Lawrence, Kansas, on how to flow together in the same way that the musicians, singers, and prayer leaders flow together in corporate intercession meetings at IHOPKC. During this time of training I was caught up in the Spirit. In this moment of encounter God revealed to me how powerful our corporate model of worship and prayer really is.

First, I saw the heavens open and I noticed dark gray clouds swirling like you would see in severe weather. In the swirling dark clouds, I was shocked to see the snarling face of the image of Ichabod appear. I discerned that this was the principality over the city of Topeka and I discerned that the angry countenance on Ichabod's face was directly related to our training up musicians, singers, and prayer leaders to flow together in this model of corporate intercession.

As the prayer leader, musicians, and singers concluded praying from Ephesians 1:17 for the Church in Topeka, the prayer leader began making a few scriptural declarations speaking out repeatedly, "Let there be light!" "Let there be light!" What occurred next was so powerful. I saw in the Spirit what I would describe as the smoke of incense arising from each of the 8 individuals on this newly formed worship team that were being trained. Next, these columns of incense joined together, funneling and becoming one stream arising to heaven. But as the prayer leader declared, "Let there be light!" this stream of united incense became a military missile. I watched this missile launch and explode dead center in the face of the angry Ichabod principality high up in the heavens. It was a direct hit too! Included with the direct hit was a loud explosion like the sound of a sonic BOOM!

The encounter ended with the sonic boom. God impressed upon my heart what is happening in the Spirit realm when we unite in worship and intercession. The context was using a team of first time rookies who had never been teamed up to worship and pray like this ever before. This fact again allowed me to understand that rookies, who don't have the worship and prayer model mastered, are more effective than they realize. This encounter has given me much hope that one day we can unite in Topeka, Kansas, release incense smart bombs day and night, and take back what the enemy has stolen.

My point is that our prayers really matter. The devil is a liar. I used to think that God is Sovereign and whatever He wants done He will get it done and my prayers don't really have much of any influence on His kingdom. I now have a revelation that every single one of my little prayers thunders in heaven! God is listening! My prayers are powerful and effective!

I acknowledge that I have had much good teaching during my time here at the International House of Prayer in Kansas City which has greatly helped me. I also now understand that for decades God has been waiting for me to pray His Word. I had had things backwards. I had thought I was waiting for the Acts 2 outpouring of the Holy Spirit to launch me into prayer and a walk of powerful signs and wonders; but I was so mistaken in my wrong thinking.

Isaiah 30:18-19 says that God is waiting to hear my cry, and that when I cry out to him that He will be very gracious at the sound of my voice and that He will answer me.

Isaiah 30, "*Therefore the* L*ORD* *will wait, that He may be gracious to you...* (v.18). "*...He will be very gracious to you at the sound of your cry; When He hears it, He will answer you* (v.19).

Why does God want us to pray? He wants us to connect with His heart in deep partnership. I challenge you to personalize Ephesians 1:17-18 and pray something similar to what I pray in the prayer below, and pray it a lot, and pray it over everything.

"God it's me again, Your favorite, the one You enjoy, the one You like, asking that You would give me, Rick Rupp, the Spirit of wisdom and revelation in the knowledge of Jesus, so that the eyes of my heart would be enlightened to know the hope of Your calling, and the riches of the glory of Your inheritance in me. Manifest what is the exceeding greatness of Your power towards us who believe in You, in me and through me."

Every day I start praying all three prayers found in the Book of Ephesians over my life (Ephesians 1:17; Ephesians 3:16; and Ephesians 6:10-18). Prior to joining the staff at IHOPKC I was not even aware that these prayers existed. This is my first golden nugget. In the next chapter let's examine another powerful life changing prayer found in Ephesians chapter 3.

Chapter 4
Golden Nugget #2

So obviously, by now you understand that when I joined IHOPKC I was a mess. I look back and thank God for His leadership in my life. On numerous occasions I've heard our IHOPKC leaders say that we are a 'greenhouse type ministry' to strengthen broken and hurting people, as I was.

I call my first 6 years at IHOPKC my season of healing. I came here so desperate for God. I spent long hours in the prayer room every day. I read the Bible from cover to cover several times. I attended every teaching session that was available. I volunteered as an usher at all our meetings. I started fasting on a regular basis. It was as if I was in an incubator of the Father's love and care to rebuild my life. At this time, God wrote the Ephesians 1 prayer on my heart.

Next, He was adding to it the Ephesians 3 prayer, which is the second gold nugget I found. God was also writing this second prayer for strength and love onto my heart. It was the second most–prayed prayer on the microphone in the IHOPKC prayer room. This prayer is found in Ephesians 3:14-20.

¹⁴ For this reason I bow my knees to the Father of our Lord Jesus Christ, ¹⁵ from whom the whole family in heaven and earth is named, ¹⁶ that He would grant you, according to the riches of His glory, to be strengthened with might through His Spirit in the inner man, ¹⁷ that Christ may dwell in your hearts through faith; that you, being rooted and grounded in love, ¹⁸ may be able to comprehend with all the saints what is the width and length and depth and height— ¹⁹ to know the love of Christ which passes knowledge; that you may be filled with all the fullness of God (Ephesians 3:14-20).

During my incubator season, I remember my heart longing for a closer, more intimate relationship with Jesus. Many times, I confessed to God that I really did not know how to pray, how to wait, or hear His voice as I should. After hearing Mike Bickle share from Isaiah 58 a message entitled *'The Lovesick Heart of the Fasted Lifestyle.'* I could not believe one of his comments. Mike said that there is a grace for enjoyable fasting. That just did not seem realistic. Could this really be true? Would God give me grace and His strength for enjoyable fasting and an intimate friendship in a place where I could hear His voice?

I felt so weak and yet something inside resonated within me to make a few lifestyle changes, and so I began praying that God would give me the strength for fasting food. I started contending for a lovesick heart and special grace to live a fasted lifestyle.

At one point, God asked me to turn off and get rid of my television which I agreed was a good decision. I replaced the TV with reading the Bible and listening to Mike Bickle teachings. Then God asked me to turn off all my sports. At that time, I never missed a Chiefs football game on TV or a Kansas Jayhawks college basketball game. So, I replaced sports with more time in the prayer room, singing and meditating on His Word.

Then to my surprise He asked me to get rid of my cell phone. My initial response was to tell God that was just not fair. I told Him that most Christians I knew had and used cell phones. God gently reminded me that one of my prayers was for a closer, more intimate relationship with Him, where

I could hear His voice. He was right. By now thousands of times I had prayed, "God, teach me to pray! God, I rarely hear Your voice! God, what are you thinking and what are You feeling?"

When I asked Him why I needed to fast from my phone God said, "Rick, you need to get rid of your cell phone because you are talking to people more than you are talking to Me. You said that you value hearing My voice above all else." He was right. I cancelled my phone service and began cultivating a continual conversation with God.

For the next few months I wore a pager, wanting to provide my three children with the ability to contact me if there was ever an emergency. But after 6 months the pager had never been used once. Instead I was given a lap top. Therefore I cancelled the pager service and to this day, 16 years later, I'm still without a cell phone and I continue to use email for communicating with people.

I remember saying, "Okay God, if I lay down all these things then this means You have to become my excitement, my adventure, and my entertainment."

One way the Lord started answering the Ephesians 3 prayer that I prayed so often was by showing His love for me in providing for my needs. A big struggle for me was money to live on. To remain a full-time intercessor at the International House of Prayer I needed monthly supporters. For whatever reason, it seemed as if everyone I invited to become a monthly financial partner said no. In other words, I was struggling to find friends and family who would send me monthly support to remain a full-time intercessor at IHOPKC. I did find another single man serving at IHOPKC to share the expense of renting my two-bedroom apartment. I visited food pantries for my groceries. Then things began to happen. For example one day a person at IHOPKC said that they were moving and they wanted to give me their high mileage Dodge van. So I sold my Camry for $3500. This enabled me to pay my expenses, while I continued to write letters and visit people that I thought would sponsor me for my full-time occupation to stand in the gap and pray.

I prayed this Ephesians 3:16 prayer much. Paul prayed this prayer for the believers in the Church at Ephesus which I was now doing too. I was praying this prayer daily for the Church in Topeka and also for other cities, but because I was facing so many personal challenges I needed to pray this prayer for myself just to survive!

I was perplexed and concerned and wondered how God would provide for my needs. I thought to myself: "God, You called me to intercession when You thundered from heaven in an audible voice and said 'Rick, now you know how I feel. My bride has done the exact same thing and she too has run off with other lovers. I am looking for a friend to stand in the gap and make intercession."

Even my Pastor had counseled me to quit my job, go to IHOPKC, and contend for the Church to move again in apostolic power. He had said, "We don't need a man who makes a lot of money, we need a man with a spirit of prayer." All this pressure forced me to the cross of Calvary. I was burning all my bridges and determined to stand on the promises of God's Word.

Everything I was going through was a divine set up. Little money meant more fasting. I remember treating myself to a $1.88 single slice of pizza at Sam's Club at the end of the month if I had the money. If I had $5 at the end of the month, I would invite one of the 20-year-old IHOPKC young men to join me for a single slice at Sam's Club, but I'd tell him that I couldn't afford the pizza combo which included a soft drink. So, it was a single slice of Sam's pizza and a free glass of water for several years as I managed to live on $700–$800 per month.

Through living and experiencing this season I can assuredly tell you that God invites us into a conversation with Him. He listens to what we have to say, no matter how insignificant we think it is, and He wants us to listen to what He answers us through His Word and from His Spirit. Praying His Word back to Him is so powerful.

One afternoon in 2004 I was sitting in the IHOPKC prayer room and I was in conversation with God. I was talking with Holy Spirit asking Him what's next. I was praying much for God to release all of the resources needed to establish His House of Prayer in Topeka, Kansas. By faith I knew that someday God would awaken others in Topeka to His heart's desire for a 24/7 expression of worship and prayer. The Holy Spirit spoke to me telling me that part of my training included doing the night watch as a lifestyle. I contacted the leader of the night watch and was offered the chance to do prayer leading for a worship team.

I officially joined the IHOPKC night watch on October 24, 2004. For 3 1/2 years from May 17, 2001 through October 24, 2004 I had been spending 12 hours a day, six days per week, in the prayer room, and sleeping at night. I would get up at 4 am so I could be in the prayer room by 5 am. But now I radically changed my sleep schedule, going to bed at 6:30 am and getting up at 1 pm. After a week, my body clock was set to this new sleep schedule and I soon discovered the night watch is really special. I tell people that my eternal resume includes my 12 1/2 years serving as a prayer leader in the night watch.

I encourage you to consider a season serving as a full-time intercessor at any House of Prayer doing the night watch, so your eternal resume also includes time at the feet of Jesus in the night. Think about this opportunity. Now may be your only chance to serve in the night watch as the return of Christ draws ever closer. The Bible says in the age to come there will not be night.

"And the city has no need of sun or moon, for the glory of God illuminates the city, and the Lamb is its light" (Revelation 21:23).

It's interesting that after switching to the night watch schedule I was able to find people to partner with me financially. I also experienced the supernatural provision of a new vehicle. The engine went out on the van I was driving. My first thought was that I was done at IHOPKC, but God heard as I cried out for Him to make a way for me to remain full time. God knew I needed a dependable vehicle to continue driving to Open Way Church in Topeka, Kansas every Sunday morning, as well as to and from our Friday night prayer watch in Topeka which we called THOP.

When I shared with my IHOPKC night watch worship team that I was without a vehicle and uncertain how long I'd remain a full-time intercessor, the worship team leader offered me his car on weekends. This meant I could drive to Topeka and back. But once my Open Way Church family in Topeka heard about my crisis vehicle situation a family gave me a 1992 Subaru, and another person at Open Way gave me $1700.00 cash saying it was for my new vehicle. I was so excited. I was thinking God was saying that He was going to provide me with more financial blessings so I could eventually get a newer van similar to the one that had died. When I shared this idea excitedly with my Pastor he gave me 'that look' and said,

"Rick, I think God wants you to have that $1700.00 for future repairs. I'm pretty sure it's not so you can get another van.

Well on my second round-trip with my Subaru gift as I was on my way home on a very hot July afternoon driving through Lawrence, Kansas, my Subaru overheated. I pulled into a parking lot and waited patiently for it to cool down. At a safe point, I added water to the radiator and expected to drive to my apartment in Kansas City, but the car would not start.

I called the person who had given the Subaru to me. He instructed me to lock the car and put the keys on top of the front tire on the driver's side. He said not to worry. He said he knew what the problem was and that he would bring his trailer to take it back to his garage and repair it. After several weeks, I had that Subaru back with a completely rebuilt engine because the head gasket had blown. But that's not the end of this God story!

I could not believe how much gas this Subaru was costing me to drive compared to my old van. I was now paying $24 each round trip from Kansas City to Topeka and I told the Lord that I needed a more economical vehicle. Two weeks later, a man in the

IHOPKC prayer room asked if he could talk to me for a few minutes. Talking is not permitted inside the prayer room so we went to another room where he shared that he wanted to sow some money into my life. He said it was for something big that I was asking from God. I told him if he wanted a tax receipt that he should make out his check to IHOPKC. Wow! Was I stunned when he handed me a check for $2400 and he made it out to Rick Rupp and not IHOPKC!

The next Sunday I showed my Pastor the $2400 check and told him that I was sure God was releasing funds so I could get myself a more economical vehicle. He said perhaps I was right but that I should forget about getting myself another van. He said I should start praying about a Honda Civic or a Toyota Corolla. I still thought to myself that a 4–cylinder van would be more economical.

So, I kept praying for His perfect vehicle. A few weeks later it happened again. A man approached me in the IHOPKC prayer room saying he needed to talk with me. Once in a room where we could talk privately, he said the Lord told him to give me a $2600 check and he also wanted to make a 12-month commitment to support me with $200 per month. I told him that I had been praying for a vehicle. I explained that if he wanted a tax receipt to make out his check to IHOPKC but again he said no and instead made out the check in my name!

I started researching what I could now purchase with the sum total I had received (less the amount I tithed to the Lord), but all the Corollas and Civics in that price range had such high mileage. I shared my car money testimony with another intercessor at IHOPKC, named Mary. She asked if I had ever written down exactly what color and features I wanted for my new vehicle. I said no that I had not, She got out her pen and paper and asked, "OK, what color do you want? How many doors, 2 or 4? Do you want AC? Do you want an automatic or manual transmission?" This was new information. No one had ever taught me of the necessity of writing down on paper a prayer list before, but I respected Mary and together we got everything down in writing.

My list included a white 4-door Corolla or Civic with Automatic Transmission, Air Conditioning and a CD player. Then she said that she would buy my Subaru, because it was an all-wheel drive which was perfect for her needs. I accepted her offer to buy my used Subaru.

So, I took my new car prayer list and showed it to one of my prayer partners and we started praying more specifically for my new vehicle. Several weeks passed and I got a letter in the mail from a Church. Some months earlier, I had invited this Church to become one of my monthly supporters and they said that they would pray about it. Inside the letter, I discovered a check for $3,000 plus a letter saying that instead of doing monthly support, the Lord had instructed them that there was something big I needed - maybe money for a missions trip or a car or something like that. The note also said that God told them to make out the check in my name and not make it payable to IHOPKC.

A week later my prayer partner tells me that his brother has been searching for either a Corolla or a Civic and that they had found a car dealer in St Joseph, MO, which had quite a few of both, at really good prices. I was invited to ride along with them—an invitation which I accepted. So, they select two Civics, one for them and one for their son, and I selected a white 4-door Toyota Corolla. My selection matched everything on my prayer list. The three-car deal resulted in an unbelievably low price for this 2005 Corolla with only 13,000 miles on it. However, I ended up being $1500 short. The dealer promised to hold the car for me for one week.

I began praying for God to speak to one more person as He had to these others. Several days later I saw the man in the prayer room who had given me the $2600.00 check and the 1-year commitment for $200.00 a month support. It took all the courage that I could muster up, but I went over and talked with him. I explained to him that I had found my 2005 Corolla but needed another $1500.00. I asked him if instead of sending me the $200.00 per month support, he could give me a $1500.00 check so I could purchase this vehicle in three days. He said that he would pray about it and let me know.

Amazingly two days later he brings me an envelope with a check and a letter that says. "Rick, the Lord told me to give you a check for $1700 , because you forgot about the cost of paying the car tax and getting your new plates. God also told me to stick with supporting you the next 12 months at $200 per month."

Several days later, my friends and I returned to St Joseph, MO to pick up our three cars! So on October 24, 2005, I am writing a huge check to purchase a

2005 Corolla with 13,000 miles which includes all the features that were on my specific prayer list and the Holy Spirit whispers, "Happy Anniversary". I paid for my new car and on the drive home it dawned on me that October 24th was my one-year anniversary of joining the IHOPKC night watch!

God was teaching me what it means to wait upon the Lord through this car experience. It started on that terribly hot day in July when my head gasket blew in the Subaru which had been given to me. This miracle Corolla encounter happened over several months. I received the 4 large sums of money from people who were all hearing from the Holy Spirit to sow into this need, plus Mary's money from purchasing my Subaru. Eventually, on October 24, 2005, a struggling prayer guy paid in full for a 2005 Toyota Corolla!

Wow! Step by step God was restoring my life. I was walking in new revelation and praying to a God who likes me. God was helping me to believe in His promises. People around me were coaching me to write down my specific prayers and wait on His provision. The blood of Jesus had set me free from the stronghold of shame that had paralyzed me as a result of the divorce. God's provision of a car increased my faith. My three children were so surprised when I showed them my fully paid Corolla and took them for a ride in it. Of course, I had been sharing with them on a weekly basis as this God story was in progress. It was a great testimony of encouragement for my night watch worship team friends, many of themselves struggling with finances to do what God has called them to do. My Pastor and friends at Open Way Church in Topeka, Kansas were stunned at this miracle Toyota that God provided!

So, do you remember that the round-trip cost for fuel from Kansas City to Topeka in the Subaru was $24? Well, I filled my Corolla tank full in Kansas City and drove to Open Way Church for our Friday night prayer meeting. Back in Kansas City I refilled my tank and discovered my new round-trip cost was $7.50!

My car adventure was proving to be one of the answers to the many times I had prayed Ephesians 3: 14-20. God was showing me the depth of His love for me in taking care of my practical needs.

My journey of contending for a spirit of prayer next led me to daily praying another prayer over myself from the book of Ephesians.

Chapter 5
Golden Nugget #3

At this point in my prayer journey I memorized Ephesians 6:10-18 and began to daily "pray on" the full armor of Christ.

¹⁰ *Finally, my brethren, be strong in the Lord and in the power of His might.* ¹¹ *Put on the whole armor of God, that you may be able to stand against the wiles of the devil.* ¹² *For we do not wrestle against flesh and blood, but against principalities, against powers, against the rulers of the darkness of this age, against spiritual hosts of wickedness in the heavenly* places. ¹³ *Therefore take up the whole armor of God, that you may be able to withstand in the evil day, and having done all, to stand.*

¹⁴ *Stand therefore, having girded your waist with truth, having put on the breastplate of righteousness,* ¹⁵ *and having shod your feet with the preparation of the gospel of peace;* ¹⁶ *above all, taking*

the shield of faith with which you will be able to quench all the fiery darts of the wicked one. ¹⁷And take the helmet of salvation, and the sword of the Spirit, which is the word of God; ¹⁸praying always with all prayer and supplication in the Spirit, being watchful to this end with all perseverance and supplication for all the saints.

I was meditating on Jesus as the "Prayer Warrior in Heaven" during my time in the IHOPKC prayer room. During that time of meditation, it dawned on me that the fasted lifestyle I was living was like being a soldier in military boot camp. However, I was not taking Paul's advice in Ephesians 6 seriously. I was not putting on the full armor of God.

So, as I was reading slowly through Ephesians 6 I decided I would personalize it into "praying on" each piece of the full armor of God. This is something I had never thought of before. I could not ever remember hearing a sermon or teaching about "praying on" the full armor of God. So, I combined the Ephesians 1:17 prayer with the Ephesians 3:16 prayer and added the Ephesians 6:10-18 prayer to my daily prayers.

Every day the first thing out of my lips were these 3 prayers found in the Book of Ephesians. I now call these three prayers "God's three golden nuggets".

I have found that my inner man is my most important aspect of life. Before coming to IHOPKC praying for myself, or praying for my inner man, had been my most neglected prayer focus. I simply had had no revelation comparable to what I was currently receiving in the corporate prayer meetings. Prior to my coming to IHOPKC I had never taken note of all the biblical prayers that are in the Bible. Now I see that these prayers are everywhere!

The fact that Jesus was revealing Himself to me as a passionate Bridegroom God who is jealous for His bride was a direct result of praying the Ephesians 1:17 prayer asking for greater revelation of who He is. I highly recommend reading Mike Bickle's book *Passion for Jesus* which started me on my personal journey of beholding Jesus as the Bridegroom God with a burning heart. As Mike Bickle says in his book… "we become what we behold".

It took me years of studying His emotions through singing and reading the Bible to discover that Jesus is for me! He likes me! Even in my weakness Jesus enjoys me! Beholding Jesus was so key in my journey to a vibrant life of communing with Him. Talking to Jesus is prayer. It is so simple. I was now discovering the tools needed to cultivate a "spirit of prayer".

Another thing that I did was make myself a daily prayer schedule. I recommend Christians schedule regular prayer times and establish prayer lists to provide focus for their scheduled prayer times. I probably had a 5 minute a day prayer life as a Christian prior to joining IHOPKC. I would guess that many others who love Jesus never develop a prayer life because they lack the two practical aspects of scheduling time and having a prayer list.

My son is a very dedicated and disciplined weight lifter. To achieve the goals that he desires he must watch what he eats. He must schedule time in the gym. His body is responding to his steady repetition of pumping weights. So, I joke with him often telling him that if he could see my inner man it would look like Arnold Schwarzenegger. You get my point? There have been a few occasions where I have been criticized for spending long hours sitting in a prayer room telling God what He tells me to tell Him.

From experience, I can tell you that cultivating a spirit of prayer takes time. Believe me I had plenty of reasons to quit. I thank God for raising up a company of people from around the nations to gather in Kansas City who, like myself, have felt this Ezekiel 22:30 calling from God to come and stand in the gap and pray for revival.

I'm approaching May 17, 2017 as I sit here typing away at writing this book and May 17 is my 16-year anniversary serving as a full-time intercessor here at IHOPKC.

My testimony is that what we are doing 24/7 here at IHOPKC is so right. It is right to love and worship Jesus day and night. Like Mary of Bethany, it is right that we waste our lives sitting at the feet of Jesus. Jesus is worthy of continuous worship and adoration, here on earth as it is in heaven. I have no regrets. I now marvel at the wisdom of God to draw me here "for such a time as this".

I can tell you there is wisdom in sitting in a chair at the IHOPKC prayer room 8 -12 hours per day. I can tell you that living a life of continuous singing, prayer, and worship will tenderize and change your heart. Even Jesus in the Lord's Prayer taught us to start with worship and say, "Hallowed be Your name".

I love to worship Jesus! I can tell you that worship will thrust us into prayer and intercession. Again, this is the model Jesus teaches us in the Lord's Prayer: first worship, then prayer. After "Hallowed be your name" we enter into praying "Your kingdom come and Your will be done". I can tell you from experience that whatever you pray for, you will fall in love with.

Try this model and see what happens. I guarantee that if you start praying for yourself using these three golden nuggets, you will start to love yourself. I guarantee that if you start praying for the church in your city with these Biblical prayers, you will fall in love with the church in your city. I guarantee that if you start praying for a nation, God will ambush your heart for that nation.

But there is another step in the progression of worship unto prayer. The third step is evangelism. In my case I fell in love with the church in the Solomon Islands and Papua New Guinea because I prayed these three prayers over these nations. I love God with all my heart. I love myself because He first loved me. And I love the poor and oppressed people in the Solomon Islands and Papua New Guinea. I love to go and share the Gospel with them.

Never in my wildest dreams did I expect to be used by Jesus to raise up His 24/7 Houses of Prayer in the Solomon Islands, to train and give unemployed locals their first job, and provide drinking water for entire villages of poor people.

In both the Solomon Islands and Papua New Guinea many people are without electricity and without the financial means to afford a water well. In 2016 our CleanWater4Life.com ministry sponsored fifty water wells.

Never in my wildest dream did I expect Jesus would use me to help build a large 2-story Orphan/Visitor House in a jungle village without electricity as we have done in Fa'arau, Solomon Islands.

We now have two Tractor Well Drill Rigs in two different Provinces of the Solomon Islands installing water wells.

Together we have started a cement block making business in Fa'arau which employees 15 local men. Because of generous partners we have held "Free for the Poor" medical clinics in both Papua New Guinea, and the Solomon Islands leading thousands to salvation in Christ.

In 2017 my prayer is to restart our "Free for the Poor" medical clinics which were put on hold in 2015 because of the untimely death of Dr Rick Bass. (See Tribute to Dr Rick Bass on page 133)

God truly has done exceedingly abundantly beyond all I was thinking and praying for in both of these South Pacific Nations. At this time I am praying for another Tractor Well Drilling Rig and resources so we can branch out and rescue the poor people needing clean drinking water in Vanuatu and other nations.

It is this model of extravagant prayer, and now unto evangelism and transformation that I want to share in the next section.

Here is my personalized prayer using the three prayers I call the Three Golden Nuggets found in Ephesians 1:17; Ephesians 3:16; and Ephesians 6:10-18.

"God it's me again, Your favorite, the one You enjoy, the one You like, asking that You would give me, Rick Rupp, the spirit of wisdom and revelation in the knowledge of Jesus. That the eyes of my heart would be enlightened to know what is the hope of Your calling, and what are the riches of the glory of me being Your inheritance, and make known to me the exceedingly greatness of Your power towards us who believe.

"Father according to the riches of Your glory strengthen me with might through Your Spirit in my inner man, so that Christ may dwell in my heart through faith, so I may be rooted and grounded in love, so I may be able to comprehend with all the saints what is the width, the length, the height, and the depth of Your love, and so I am filled with all the fullness of God.

"And God I pray on the Ephesians 6:10-18 full armor of God. Please make Rick Rupp strong in the Lord and in the power of Your might. Having done all that I would stand in the evil days. Yes, that I would stand against the wiles of the devil for we wrestle not against flesh and blood but against principalities, powers, rulers of darkness of this age, or spiritual hosts of wickedness in heavenly places. I pray on the belt of truth, the breast plate of righteousness, my feet are shod with the preparation of the Gospel of peace, most of all I take up the shield of faith and quench every fiery dart of the enemy, I pray on the helmet of salvation, and I take up the sword of the Spirit which is the Word of God and find Rick Rupp praying always making prayers and supplications in the Spirit, and being watchful with grace to pray for all the saints."

Sometimes I also personalize this prayer and tack on Psalm 134 by praying:

"And being watchful with grace to pray for all the saints, with grace to make You known, with grace to behold and bless You as a servant of the Lord who stands by night in the house of the Lord, lifting up my hands in Your sanctuary to bless You. Abba, it is written that You will bless me out of Zion. The Lord bless you, Rick Rupp, and keep you. The Lord make His face to shine upon you and be gracious unto you. The Lord lift up the light of His countenance upon you Rick and give you shalom (peace).

To end this chapter let me share the following quote from *God's Answer to the Growing Crisis* by Mike Bickle (page 110)

"For a model of how to develop a life of prayer, we need look no further than Jesus. Each time we find Him praying in the Gospels, we get a better sense of His relationship with the Father- which is the foundation of prayer. The love shared between the Father and Son is profound. We too can speak His promises back to Him with confidence (faith) and affection (love). Intercession includes "standing in the gap" for someone, something, or some situation (Ezekiel 22:30). It involves intentionally petitioning God according to His promises, so as to release and enact His will on the earth.

According to Hebrews 7:25 what is Jesus doing full time? He spends His time and energy asking the Father for that which has been spoken to Him by the Father, and yet the Father has said He will not release anything except in partnership with Jesus and in response to His church's asking Him. What an incredible picture of humility, submission, obedience, partnership, and love- and yet what a remarkable reality!

Through Jesus' example we see that prayer is not merely rote words; it is the Spirit-empowered language of heaven. By declaring what the Father declares and partnering with His Holy Spirit, the church engages in a spiritual war in which the victor and the victory are already assured."*[1]

---

[1] Permission granted.

Section 3

Healing The Land

Building Bridges

Miracles, Provision And Water

Branching Out

More Bridges

Rick Bass

Chapter 6
Healing The Land

Now I get to share some of the fruit of burning all my bridges and joining IHOPKC in 2001. After spending long hours at the feet of Jesus contending for a spirit of prayer, God began building His bridge to the South Pacific Islands.

Warning: this is dangerous prayer! Somewhere in 2006 I started talking to Holy Spirit about this Bible verse in 2 Chronicles 7:14:

"If My people who are called by My name will humble themselves, and pray and seek My face, and turn from their wicked ways, then I will hear from heaven, and will forgive their sin and heal their land."

I knew that the power of Jesus' blood qualified me as one of those referred to in the phrase "My people who are called by My name". I had come to IHOPKC and spent much time searching my heart and repenting of my pride and arrogance, so this was a time of humbling myself. I confessed my prayerlessness as sin, and was praying more than ever. I was purposely shutting down the things that had, for years, prevented me from seeking Jesus as the prize of my life. By the grace of God, I was turning from my wicked ways, my compromise, and everything that kept me from walking in the first commandment. And now I was asking Jesus for the evidence of the things I was hoping for, in regards to His promise to hear, to forgive, and to heal the land. However, I had no grid to understand what "heal their land" meant or would look like.

I began praying: "Dear God I have no grid for what 2 Chronicles 7:14 means. I have never seen or experienced this healing of the land that You promise. Please help me take all the necessary steps of humbling myself, being a man of prayer, seeking Your face wholeheartedly, and turning from my wicked ways. Father I desire to experience the reality of 2 Chronicles 7:14."

I was very inspired by George Otis Junior's visits to IHOPKC. He had much to share about this verse, with powerful stories and testimonies from Fiji of actual healing of the land. I had to know more. I obtained some of his Transformation DVD's and watched them several times.

I contacted George Otis Junior, through his web site, to ask about joining one of the healing of the land tours, and found out that there was still room for me if I could raise $2500.00 to pay for his trip package. Immediately I began praying for $2500.00 so I could visit Fiji for this 10-day conference scheduled at the end of August 2008.

I will never forget the unfolding of this testimony of God's provision for my Fiji trip. I was sitting in the front row of the IHOPKC prayer room and Misty Edwards was leading the 4 pm worship and intercession meeting. My arms were raised in worship and this guy walks in front of me and slips a check into my shirt pocket. As he walks by he whispers in my ear "Cash it quick". I'm thinking it's probably a $50 check to help me with some groceries or to help me put some gas in my miracle Corolla, but to my surprise it was exactly $2500! Wow! Wow! Wow! It was confirmation that God was sending me to Fiji! I was so excited! "Thank You, Jesus for Your provision for my trip! Wow! I'm going to Fiji! I am going to witness healing of the land in Fiji!"

I went home and told my roommate, a young man from Finland, who was renting a bedroom from me for 6 months, while he was doing the IHOPKC night watch. His name was Mikko and he had been to the Solomon Islands. He suggested we contact a Solomon Island friend that he thought was in his final year of Bible school in Fiji. We sent off an email to his friend Freddie Mannie and discovered that Freddie had graduated from the Fiji Bible School and was currently in Jefferson City, MO, leading worship at a summer youth camp as part of his Bible School externship program.

Since Jefferson City is only three hours from Kansas City, I emailed Freddie an invitation to come, stay at my house, and visit the IHOPKC prayer room. Freddie returned my email saying that his heart leapt when he read my email invitation. He said that he heard the Holy Spirit whisper: "Freddie you thought you were coming to the USA to lead worship for this church's youth camp externship but I brought you here to introduce you to the 24/7 prayer and worship at IHOPKC." We were delighted that Freddie had a few days free in his schedule to come for a visit.

I purchased Freddie a round trip bus ticket and soon he and I were sitting together doing the

IHOPKC night watch. Freddie was reading a Mike Bickle book that I had lent him called "The Pleasures of Loving God". It was 3 am and the night watch worship leader Sarah Edwards was singing her song "Dark but Lovely". Between the Song of Solomon theme in Mike's book and the lyrics of Sarah's song it was as if a lightning bolt of revelation of God's heart hit Freddie's heart! With big eyes Freddie looked over at me and said "Rick, my people in the Solomon Islands have never heard of the revelation that God enjoys us, that Jesus is a Bridegroom God who likes us, and that His desire is for us! Rick, please, you must come home with me to my village in the Solomon Islands and share this Song of Solomon revelation. Come and share that that although we are dark, God says that we are beautiful! We are very religious people but this revelation will change everything in the Solomon Islands!"

I explained to Freddie that it would be very unlikely that I could raise the additional $1500 for the airfare to come first to the Solomon Islands and then go on to Fiji. However, I told him I would send out an email invitation and see what God would do. Freddie agreed to pray and fast for me to receive the additional funds so I could include a week in Solomon Islands prior to my time in Fiji. Much to my delight, two people responded to my email request and exactly the right amount of money came in, allowing me to travel first to the Solomon Islands and from there fly to Fiji in August 2008.

It is interesting that the same revelation that had changed everything for me had now deeply touched Freddie Mannie too. I pray everyone reading this book will experience this same life changing revelation.

At mikebickle.org there is a free library containing all Mike Bickle's teaching sessions. I recommend his numerous teachings on experiencing God's affections. I also recommend reading all the books written by Mike Bickle.

Here are the lyrics to Sarah's "Dark but Lovely" song that God used to impact Freddie.*[2]

I can't understand, this work of grace
How a perfect God would come and take my place
The stars they don't move You
The waves can't undo You
The mountains in their splendor
They cannot steal Your heart
This God who is holy, perfect in beauty

---

[2] Permission granted.

Awesome in glory is ravished by my heart

Though I'm poor, You say I am lovely
Though I'm dark, You say I'm beautiful

Somehow my weak glance has overwhelmed You
And somehow my weak love has stolen away Your
heart

Sarah's song unpacks the scripture verse from Song of Solomon 4:9:

"You have ravished my heart, my sister, my spouse; you have ravished my heart with one look of your eyes, with one jewel of your necklace."

Soon the time arrived for 26 year old Freddie Mannie, a worship leader/intercessor from the Solomon Islands, and I to travel. We boarded our flight from Kansas City to Honiara, the capital of the Solomon Islands. After spending two nights in Honiara we went aboard a transport ship with hundreds of Solomon Islanders and proceeded to the village of Fa'arau on the Island of Malaita, where Freddie was born.

The voyage from Honiara, which is located on the Island named Guadalcanal, took approx. 5 hours.

We arrived at Port Auki on the island of Malaita but there was a problem. There was no available dock space at the wharf to unload several hundred of us. Obviously, the captain had been in this predicament before. He pulled our ship alongside another big ship and the people started jumping onto this adjoining ship and then onto the wharf. What a sight to behold! From my perspective, it was mass chaos. Once I had navigated this rather tricky disembarkation with my luggage in hand there was an old yellow jeep waiting to transport me from Port Auki to the village of Fa'arau.

This was my first time to witness rural village life in the Solomon Islands. Fa'arau is a typical village of approximately 300 people of which 90 are children and youth. Each family relies on their gardens to survive. These were poor people without jobs and without money. I noticed that everyone had sweet potatoes growing in their gardens. We ate mostly home-grown fruits and vegetables. The climate is hot and humid year around. Some families have metal roofs on their primitive dwellings and they catch rain water for drinking and bathing in metal drums and buckets. Many of their homes have thatched roofs that they make from bush materials. There were no toilets. You figure that one out. At night, we used kerosene lanterns for lighting both in the Church and in their homes. Everyone did their cooking over open wood fires. The people of Fa'arau shared one vehicle for community use which, once you pushed to get it started, got us where we needed to go. Fuel was expensive at $10 per gallon. I slept on a mat on the floor since no one had beds like the ones I was used to back home. I needed just a sheet to cover me because the temperature only dropped to 75 degrees most nights. Wow! I was living with people who are quite happy and yet they lived without electricity, refrigerators, washing machines and the many comforts that I was accustomed to.

I noticed that some of the people from Fa'arau could speak and understand English but not everyone. Their accent when speaking English made me really listen in order to catch what they were saying. On occasions, I had to ask them to repeat what they had said to me. English is the national language and is used in their schools. Little children 6 years old and younger could not understand or speak English because they had not started school. The 50-year olds and older could not speak much English because many had either dropped out of school or never went to school. However, I discovered that this older group could understand my English but just lacked the confidence to answer me in English. I was thankful that Freddie was there with me to help whenever there was a language issue.

I was glad to have this opportunity of visiting Fa'arau even though my living conditions were the most rustic that I had ever experienced. I enjoyed my visit due to the hospitality and friendliness of all the people, that made me feel so welcome. My first night in the Fa'arau Church they sang a beautiful welcome song and presented me with a handmade flower wreath that smelled amazing! The majority of their worship songs were sung in English so I could understand the words. I was surprised by the quality of their voices. Man, they were good singers! Their worship lasted for over an hour, and sometimes it lasted 2 hours. There were several times during the worship when the entire congregation of 200 would break spontaneously into intense corporate intercession. I call it the Korean style of intercession, when everyone prays together loudly and fervently for 5 – 10 minutes. Then we went right back into a worship song. I was in my element! It was so much fun to worship and pray with them. During this short visit, we met every night in the Church and every night they asked me to share something from God's Word.

I must admit that it was the first Church service I had experienced, where two kerosene lanterns were our only source of light. Everyone was barefoot. Most did not wear shoes, but a few had flip flops which were left just outside the entrance of the Church. I noticed that the only musical instruments were two very inexpensive acoustic guitars. I thanked God for allowing me to experience this one time visit to the Solomon Islands. I reminded myself that the main reason for this trip was to experience the healing of the land transformation that was taking place in Fiji. Oh, was I ever looking forward to my Fiji portion of this trip!

It was my final night with the people in the jungle village of Fa'arau. We were gathered in Fa'arau Church for our final service before Freddie would be taking me back to Honiara Airport for my flight to Fiji. After our usual several hours of worship and prayer Pastor Albert asked me if we could do a prophetic act. His request kind of surprised me so I asked him exactly what he wanted to do. Pastor Albert asked me to link hands, with him on my left and Elder Jeptha on my right. So, I stood in the middle of these two church leaders and we linked our hands. Pastor Albert then requested that I bow my head and pray to God, asking Him how He, God, would have me link together with the Church at Fa'arau. You must understand that it was never my intention to return to the Solomon Islands. I was only thinking about my next exciting trip, going to Fiji to witness healing of the land, so frankly, returning to Fa'arau had never even entered my mind. It was a bit awkward for me but I bowed my head and silently prayed: "God do you want me to link together with the church here in Fa'arau?" The crystal-clear voice of God spoke to me saying "Rick, if you will help them build a bridge in the natural, then I will build a bridge in the Spirit, and I'll birth a 24/7 House of Prayer right here in this jungle village of Fa'arau."

The next morning at sun rise I walked up the dirt path to the only bridge leading into Fa'arau village with my digital camera so I could check out and possibly photograph the condition of the bridge. Wow! Was I shocked! Their wooden bridge was rotten and frankly U-shaped. It was not safe for any vehicle to drive across. I pondered what God was asking me. The next thing I know is that I am lifting my hands towards heaven and shouting, as if God were deaf, saying, "God I am a prayer guy with no money! Why would you ask me to help them build a new bridge? Why wouldn't you give this ministry assignment to someone in marketplace ministry who has money in the bank?

I remember that at the time of my outburst, heaven was silent. And I really think Jesus had a big smile on His face looking down at me. So, I took several photos of their rotten, wooden, U-shaped, 20-foot-long bridge, which was ready to collapse at any time.

Yes, I enjoyed my time in Fiji. In fact, I had a divine appointment with a delegation of Church leaders from Papua New Guinea who were attending the healing of the land conference and tour, which I'll share about in the coming pages. Yes, God confirmed His Word concerning the power of prayer, and humility and repentance that produced healing of the land. My faith increased and now I knew that 2 Chronicles 7:14 works. During my Fiji trip, I visited 10 transformed villages and it was life changing to see and hear the wonderful testimonies. But I knew my ministry assignment was to help the village of Fa'arau build a bridge in the natural and that God had promised me He would build a bridge in the Spirit and establish His House of Prayer in the Islands.

Chapter 7
Building Bridges

When I returned home to Kansas City in September of 2008 the priority for me was raising funds to help Fa'arau build a new bridge, plus sharing about our miracle working God. I had many healing of the land testimonies! My friend Andy Blake met with me, and together we made a power point presentation so I could give slide show presentations of the rotten bridge and speak about my trip to both the Solomon Islands and Fiji. Several months later, in November, I headed to Ohio, and Michigan to visit churches, houses of prayer, and several home group type meetings for a 10-day ministry trip, to raise funds.

Again, God confirmed His word and I received the exact amount of money needed to help Fa'arau build a new bridge. The money was wired to the Fa'arau Church. The first step for them was to pay a deposit for the one and only bulldozer on the island of Malaita, and to wait for their turn. When it was their turn the bulldozer was used to transport three, thirty-foot-long hardwood tree trunks which were approximately three feet in diameter, to the bridge job site.

The bulldozer was needed to set the heavy trees into place after tearing out the rotten bridge. After that the Fa'arau men milled lumber with a rented chain saw to build the top of their new bridge. When I returned in March 2009 the bridge had been built. It was a strong and very well built bridge. I reminded them how God had spoken to me at the church service during the prophetic act of linking hands saying, "Rick if you will help them build a bridge in the natural, I will build a bridge in the Spirit and I'll birth a 24/7 House of Prayer right here in this jungle village of Fa'arau."

When I challenged them to consider starting an all-night prayer meeting, since that was the coolest time to be in their church, they responded "Oh Papa Ricky, one month before you come here, we started the 24/7 House of Prayer." It was a marvelous moment! I had done my part and helped empower Fa'arau to build a new bridge and God had done His part by stirring the hearts of the people in Fa'arau to worship and pray to Jesus day and night. They called themselves Fa'HOP Mission Base.

Later on, the leaders of Fa'HOP Mission Base told me that before my first visit to their village with Freddie Mannie that they had been asking the Holy Spirit for clarity on what Amos 9:11 meant.

"On that day I will raise up
The tabernacle of David, which has fallen down,
And repair its damages;
I will raise up its ruins,
And rebuild it as in the days of old."

It really provoked the people in Fa'arau to hear my personal testimony. I explained to them my full-time occupation at IHOPKC was ministry to the Lord in the spirit of the tabernacle of King David. I shared how King David in 1 Chronicles 25: 6-7 paid 288 singers to minister day and night for 33 years as their full-time occupation.

"All these were under the direction of their father to sing in the house of the LORD, with cymbals, harps and lyres, for the service of the house of God. Asaph, Jeduthun and Heman were under the direction of the king. [7] Their number who were trained in singing to the LORD, with their relatives, all who were skillful, was 288."

Plus, not only did King David supply funding for 288 full time singers, but he also established and funded 4,000 musicians and 4,000 gatekeepers (See 1 Chronicles 23:5; 25:7). I was amazed at how God had them searching the scriptures for understanding to the Amos 9:11 prophecy prior to me ever coming. And now the Holy Spirit was inviting these people in a jungle village that nobody knew about to sing to Jesus day and night.

After my first one week visit to the village of Fa'arau, my friend Freddie Mannie and I took the 5-hour boat ride back to the Capital City of Honiara. Freddie arranged for me to visit his Uncle Meshack, a prophet of God, since I had an extra day before my flight would depart for Fiji.

We arrived after dark. Meshack was sitting in his small, jungle bush type house with several kerosene lanterns dimly lighting his rustic dwelling. Meshack asked if he could share with me about a God encounter that he had had some 15-20 years prior to my visit in 2008. Meshack explained he had heard the audible voice of God during a 40-day water fast in which he was alone up on top of a place he called prayer mountain.

During this fast the Lord spoke to him in an audible voice saying:

"In the last days I will raise up My 24/7 prayer houses in every nation, tongue, and tribe. And the way that pastors receive their money for shepherding the sheep is the same way that the intercessors will receive money for praying. I will raise up my full-time prayer warriors and give them monies that they need so they can minister to Me in My prayer houses praying day and night."

Then Meshack looks at me and says, "Brother Ricky what do you do for your monies back in America?" I answered Meshack, "I raise my financial support from people in America which allows me to serve as a full-time intercessor at the International House of Prayer in Kansas City." But Meshack did not understand what I was trying to tell him and he responded. "No Ricky I don't think you understand my question. I'm asking you Ricky what do you do for your monies? What is your occupation?" I smiled and reworded my statement back to Meshack and said, "People pay me to pray, so that I can be a full-time prayer warrior in the 24/7 Prayer House in Kansas City." Oh, I wish you could have been there to witness the next expression on Meshack's face! His jaw dropped as he gasped saying, "Then it is happening! Ricky, we must be in the last days if God is filling His Prayer Houses with Prayer Warriors and is paying them to pray!"

Chapter 8
Miracles, Provision And Water

In 2010, when I returned to Fa'arau, I was accompanied by a team of six young people. We came expecting to have a youth conference. However, I was told by the Fa'HOP Mission Base leadership team that there were over 300 young people wanting to come to Fa'arau during our 2 weeks visit but there was not enough drinking water and no place to accommodate them. Well, it broke my heart that 300 young adults had to be refused and were unable to come to Fa'arau. Our team was kept busy with the 90 children living in Fa'arau, teaching Bible stories, doing skits, and learning new songs. Each night everyone in Fa'arau village met from 7 pm to midnight for corporate worship/prayer and preaching/teaching.

I began observing the women and children walking 2 miles to the river with their plastic containers to fetch drinking water and then walk 2 miles from the river back to their homes carrying heavy 40-pound containers on their shoulders. Because it was so hot and humid these people would walk to the river either early in the morning or right before dark in the evening. When I visited the river, I discovered the women washing their clothes and bathing. Fetching their water was a daily routine. Even 5-year-old children were carrying 2-liter bottles of water home from the river.

The Holy Spirit revealed my second ministry assignment as I was watching old women and these small children carrying their heavy loads of water. He said to me, "Rick, it is not okay with Me that My people here in Fa'arau are drinking water from the river. Help them drill a water well."

With the help of my friend Andy Blake, we put together a power point slide show presentation to explain our vision to get Fa'arau a clean source of drinking water. I secured a price to hire a well driller in Honiara which involved him bringing his 10 ton truck well drilling rig on a big barge to Fa'arau. The price was $8,000 US. For me to raise this much money seemed impossible. My yearly income living on missionary support was not much more than that. I mailed out newsletters, I emailed e-newsletters, and wherever I was invited I shared my slide show presentations, at churches, home groups, and Houses of Prayer. I organized two weekly prayer meetings with IHOPKC young people and we contended for funding to provide Fa'arau with a water well.

By the spring of 2011 after a year of fund raising I had $10,000 in the bank for the Fa'arau water well project. I put all $10,000 into a bank in the Solomon Islands earmarked for this project. The Honiara well drilling company would receive $4,000 when his rig arrived at the village of Fa'arau and the final $4,000 would be released upon completion of their water well. The other $2,000 was set aside for purchasing a tank and miscellaneous plumbing materials. However, over the next 5 months, the Honiara well driller made excuse after excuse as to why there was a delay for drilling a well in Fa'arau. I was so frustrated that I took it to the Lord in prayer.

I cried out to God saying, "God what is going on here? Surely this must be spiritual warfare because You are more committed to this water well project for Your people in Fa'arau than I am!" In that moment of being utterly frazzled God spoke to me saying, "Rick, thank you for talking to Me about this project again but listen to Me. Rick, you only got half of my heart. Yes, I want Fa'arau to drink clean water from a well but there is more to my plan. I want them to become the first well drilling company on the Island of Malaita. There are so many other villages that are desperate for clean drinking water."

My response was, "God I am just a prayer guy with no money and with no knowledge in well drilling. Why wouldn't you give a ministry assignment like this to a marketplace guy with lots of money in the bank?"

Again, as with the first assignment of the building of the bridge project, heaven was silent and I discerned the smile of Jesus saying "Come on little prayer guy, I am with you in this."

I did my research and found a company called Hydra Fab that manufactured a trailer well drilling rig. I obtained from them a list of other items necessary to start a well drilling business including the cost of sending everything inside a 20-foot container from a USA port to Port Honiara.

Deep down I knew this mountain could be conquered using God's secret weapons and that this called for an extravagant time of worship, prayer, and fasting. As I was in the IHOPKC prayer room reading and meditating on the "by faith" assignments found in Hebrews chapter 11, it came to my mind to organize a sacred assembly in Topeka, Kansas for 42 hours starting on 11/11/11 and concluding with taking up an offering for the poor on 11/13/11.

I gathered a group of Topeka House of Prayer leaders and several local pastors to ask for their support and help. In this group, it was decided to unite and call this 11/11/11 – 11/13/11 sacred assembly "Contending for the Glory" We successfully organized nonstop worship and prayer, along with nonstop Bible reading, and Kirk Bennet, from IHOPKC, agreed to do 5 teachings at this 3-day gathering. By the grace of God, I led the night watch and when I left to go sleep a few hours there were other Topeka leaders to assist. On Saturday afternoon, approximately 70 young adults from IHOPKC One Thing Internship arrived to participate in leading worship and intercession. We had worship teams from Topeka, Lawrence, Salina, Manhattan, and Wichita Kansas come to participate. Much to my delight everyone agreed that we should take up an offering for the poor on Sunday 11/13/11 and put it towards the Fa'arau water well project!

God blessed our "Contending for the Glory" sacred assembly. People from all over the State of Kansas participated. At the Sunday morning meeting, there were 5 different congregations represented. Pastor Aaron Lagani the leader of the 24/7 Fa'arau House of Prayer shared prior to us taking up an offering for his village. It was his first ever visit to the United States of America and the first time that he had ever flown on an airplane.

The amount of the offering for the Fa'arau well drill machine from that 11/13/11 service was $3,000. Now I needed another $17,000 by year-end so everything could be shipped after the first of the year in 2012. So, I started one of those "end-of-the-year" fund raising programs. I used Facebook, I sent email invitations, and shared with everyone that by December 31 we only needed $17,000 more to purchase a Hydra Fab trailer well drilling rig, plus supplies, which included the cost of shipping, to birth the first well drilling business on the Island of Malaita, Solomon Islands.

From Nov 13 to Dec 13 the original $3,000 doubled and grew to $6,000. Then a family emailed me on Dec 14, 2011 saying that they had been saving money specifically for a "helping the poor" project. God spoke to them to offer me up to a $5,000 matching gift with a time limit through the end of the year. In other words, if I were to raise only $3,000 by year's end, then they would send only $3,000 but if $5,000 were contributed then they would send me the full $5,000 for this project!

My faith skyrocketed and my efforts increased on Facebook and bulk emails. On December 30, 2011, I emailed the family who made the matching gift offer to show them that I had received $5,000 since their Dec 14 offer, not including a penny of the $6,000 that had been given from Nov 13 through Dec 13. I was now only a few thousand dollars short. Wow! I had $16,000 of the $20,000 goal on December 30.

On December 31, I was volunteering at the IHOPKC "One Thing Conference" as an usher in the main auditorium for the evening service and God told me to go an hour early and prayer walk the main auditorium. I saw the hand of God move as I circled the auditorium. Numerous times people came up to me with a check or cash saying that they had seen my Facebook posts and that they wanted to sow! Before the clock struck midnight, I had not only met my $20,000 goal, I actually went over the goal by several thousand dollars!

I still had one final very critical step yet to accomplish before we could send the 20-foot container with everything required to start a well drilling business, including enough materials to install three water wells. We needed a 100% tax and duty-free exemption from the Solomon Islands government because I had no extra money to pay these fees. Pastor Aaron Lagani applied for the exemption and after much prayer, in March 2012, the Solomon Islands officials granted the 100% exemption. It took 60 days shipping time by ocean vessel from the USA to Port Honiara and our 20-foot container arrived on June 1, 2012. I was told by Pastor Aaron that several Solomon Islands Members of Parliament were present when the Hydra Fab Trailer Well Drilling Rig was unloaded at the wharf in Honiara, Solomon Islands. He said that they asked what this machine was and where it had come from. Pastor Aaron explained it was a well drilling machine headed for Malaita to start a kingdom well drilling business and that it was a gift from the USA. They responded by saying to Aaron, "This is a historic moment for our nation. Never, in the history of the Solomon Islands, has any nation sent a well drilling machine to rescue our people in need of drinking water."

The other miracles that God provided in order to make this project a success included, Rev Kwon a Korean American that I had met at the IHOPKC night watch. He agreed to join our team and train the Fa'arau men in the art of well drilling. I certainly had no clue how to install water wells. We also needed a solar pumping system and I had no money and no knowledge of how to install a solar water pump. God met this need by using Facebook to connect me to a prayer ministry in Australia called Generation Fire. They contacted me saying that they wanted to get involved and asked if there was anything that they could supply for this project! I asked them if they knew anything about solar systems and or plumbing. It just so happened that Bob Crockford and his son Tim were engineers who specialized in water plumbing and solar projects! Wow! My ears could hardly believe it when these prayer leaders offered to raise the money needed to purchase a solar pumping system and raise the money to send a team to install the plumbing and solar system! Our final obstacle was finding one mile of PVC pipe to carry the clean drinking water from the new water well into the village of Fa'arau. It was a lot of work but with the cooperation of most of the people living in Fa'arau we were able to retrieve the PVC pipe we needed from an abandoned water line which was buried in the ground. This buried PVC pipe was actually on Fa'arau land. Approximately 20 years earlier the pipes had carried water from a spring to Fa'arau. I thank God that His Word says that when we seek first the Kingdom of God and His righteousness that all these things will be added to us (Matthew 6:33).

Our International team from the USA, Australia, Korea, and the Solomon Islands accomplished our project of installing a safe clean, water well in the village of Fa'arau. At the same time this water well project also served as the training the Fa'arau men needed so they could become the first water well business on the island of Malaita! Rev Kwon trained 6 intercessors from the Fa'arau House of Prayer in the art of installing water wells. We accomplished our goals and on September 7, 2012 the village of Fa'arau was drinking water from their new well.

Between my sending a few bulk emails with pictures, and my Facebook posts with pictures of this successful water well project at Fa'arau, I was invited by Al Caperna to speak at a gathering of marketplace entrepreneurs when I returned home to Kansas City on September 20, 2012. At this "Call 2 All" gathering of businessmen and women I was asked to share a 20-minute slide show presentation about this Fa'arau well drilling project. I was told the plan was for me to share 20 minutes and then another 20 minutes was allowed for people to comment or ask questions.

After my 20-minute Solomon Island slide show report I fielded 30 minutes' worth of questions and comments from this group of marketplace men and women. One of those in attendance asked me about additional or more similar water projects. I explained that with additional funding our vision was to establish more House of Prayer; build more water wells for villages, schools, churches, and clinics; and also to build an Orphan/Visitor House in Fa'arau; but that I had no money. The response was staggering for a prayer guy with no money. From one person attending that meeting I was given a much-needed gift of a 501(c)(3) charity status so people could now receive tax deductible receipts for contributions. Better still it came with a person who would volunteer all of their time to manage the contributions and take care of all the accounting and filing responsibilities FREE! Now 100% of contributions go to our projects since we have no administrative overhead. Because God blessed my 20 minute slide show, by year-end $100,000.00 was contributed from people attending that (Call 2 All) meeting. We originally called my new 501(c)(3) my "PNG and Solomon Islands Well and Prayer Fund" Since 2015 our name has changed to "Clean Water 4 Life PNG and Solomon Islands Fund".

My dear friend Al Caperna from Bowling Green, Ohio said that he had been praying Luke 2:52 over my life. And now it is one of my favorite prayers to pray for myself and for others.

"And Jesus increased in wisdom and stature, and in favor with God and men." Luke 2:52.

Personally, I would pray: "Dear God I want to be just like Jesus increasing in wisdom and stature, and in favor with God and man. I pray in Jesus name. Amen."

I thanked Al Caperna for his prayers and then told him that I wanted to steward this unusual favor by walking in a spirit of excellence.

The favor and blessing of God continued to increase. During my 2013 Solomon Islands ministry trip I met Jenny Hagger, the director of the Australian House of Prayer for All Nations. We both attended the Launching of the House of

Prayer in Honiara, Solomon Islands. Jenny Hagger was one of the speakers at this July 11-14, 2013 event organized by Roy Funu. I spent time sharing with Jenny about the Fa'arau House of Prayer that was established in 2009. I also shared with her my vision to help the poor and oppressed people obtain clean drinking water wells. A year later I was invited to speak at the Australian House of Prayer in Adelaide, Australia. I will later share some very significant miracles that occurred in 2015 as a result of connecting with Jenny Hagger.

In April of 2014 another 20-foot container was sent to the Fa'arau House of Prayer which contained a 32 hp Yan Mar Diesel 4-wheel drive Tractor with a PTO driven well drilling rig. Inside the container, we included a Cement Block Making Machine and a PTO driven cement mixer. By the amazing grace of God, we obtained another 100% import exemption.

Our well drilling business prior to receiving this tractor well drilling rig had been using a well rig that was mounted onto a trailer. But Fa'arau did not have a 4-wheel drive vehicle to transport the original trailer rig we sent in 2012 and so it was always a struggle with the cost of hiring a 4-wheel drive vehicle. Plus, the original trailer rig used a gasoline engine which often consumed 10 gallons of gasoline per water well. We soon discovered that our new 32 hp diesel tractor rig solved these issues. The 4-wheel drive tractor only used 3 gallons of fuel per water well and eliminated the hassle of hiring a vehicle. The cost per gallon for fuel in the Solomon Islands is $10 US. So, our goal of providing water wells at the lowest possible cost was solved using this new 32 hp diesel tractor rig.

The Cement Block Making Machine proved to be a game changer. Because there is no electricity in Fa'arau, it uses a small diesel engine to make the blocks. It also has two different block molds. Fa'arau men could now make quality 6" or 8" concrete blocks with this machine.

In 2011 the village of Fa'arau had started constructing a 40 ft X 60 ft 2-story Orphan/Visitor House. Now they were empowered to make the 3200 concrete blocks that were needed for the exterior and interior walls of the lower floor. The PTO driven cement mixer attached to the tractor enabled them to mix cement for pouring the 40 ft X 60 ft concrete floor. To obtain sand for the block making machine the tractor would go to a river located 1 mile from the Orphan/Visitor House. The tractor has a front-end loader to load river gravel and sand onto a truck. In one day, they can haul 15 truckloads of sand and gravel from the river to the block machine, which is located near the Orphan/Visitor House. It takes several more days to sift all that gravel until only the fine sand remains. From the pile of sifted sand, they can make 500 quality concrete blocks a day until they need more sand. Then they repeat the process.

So, in 2014 we birthed the first cement block making business on the Island of Malaita in Fa'arau, which was first used to produce 3500 cement blocks to build the Orphan/Visitor House. Cement blocks have now been sold to build several schools and other ongoing construction projects. This new business has given 12 men a small income and provided much needed funding to purchase diesel fuel for the Fa'arau House of Prayer generator.

Our 20-foot container also included 6 electric power tools, a generator, and a few cordless tools. My ministry partner, Benjamin Troyer, had much fun training up the Fa'arau men in the skills for framing and all facets of using power tools for the Orphan/Visitor House. We also empowered Fa'arau with two Stihl Chain Saws and milling equipment to harvest local lumber.

During this time, I heard the Lord say that it was time to branch out. I understood Him to be saying that so many other islands are desperate for clean drinking water and that He wanted me to start contending in prayer for another tractor. I also knew that God wanted to raise up many more Houses of Prayer in the South Pacific Islands. I shared this new ministry assignment with everyone at the Fa'arau Misson Base and they told me that if God provided another tractor well drilling machine to branch out to other remote islands, that they were willing and eager to go. This became a matter of prayer. It seemed impossible because now I was again out of money. I began corresponding with Dennis McAdam's, a missionary living in the Western Province. Dennis invited me to bring our house of prayer men and well drilling ministry to help the people in Munda. It was in the place of prayer that the Munda project was birthed.

The IHOPKC leadership recognized the calling on my life to minister in the South Pacific Islands and each time I would go to Daniel Lim, (the IHOPKC CEO) about needing a special leave of absence, he agreed and has been very supportive. Open Way Church in Topeka, Kansas (my home church) is also very supportive in both prayer coverage and financial support.

Chapter 9
Branching Out

In 2015 the miracles were monthly. The favor and blessing of God for this new branching-out assignment to help the poor in Munda, needing water and needing Jesus, increased way beyond anything I could have imagined.

January 2015, started out with Hydra Fab Manufacturing donating one of their PTO driven well drilling rigs for tractors. This activated my faith to trust that God would supply the tractor and the finances to pay for the cost of shipping a 20' container from the US to the Solomon Islands with everything needed to mobilize the Fa'arau Well Drilling Team to Munda, Savo, and many more islands desperate for clean drinking water!

February 2015, Jenny Hagger the director of the Australian House of Prayer for All Nations felt led of the Holy Spirit to partner with me and promote my ministry in the South Pacific Islands. Now tax-deductible receipts are given for Australians who contribute using CleanWater4Life.com.au via the Australian House of Prayer for All Nations!

March 2015, a Christian Web Page Designer from Australia contacted me saying the Holy Spirit spoke to him about producing web sites, at no cost, to help fund my ministry! He provided CleanWater4Life.com and CleanWater4Life.com.au and he designed my Facebook Page called Clean Water 4 Life. Amazing timing!

April 2015, the senior leadership team at IHOPKC featured my CleanWater4Life video on the IHOPKC Facebook Page. Over 70,000 people watched this 2-minute video! And on April 2, Rick Bass, Larry Gardner and I purchased our airfare for May 31 - July 2 ministry in Papua New Guinea!

May 2015, 27 days before our scheduled trip to Papua New Guinea, my dear friend and ministry partner Doctor Rick Bass died in a motorcycle accident in Texas on Monday May 4, 2015. Many people cried out in prayer believing that God could supply another doctor for our May 31st – July 2 trip. God answered our prayers and 10 days after the passing of Doctor Rick Bass I heard from Doctor

John Foote from Adelaide, Australia, who offered to help. Someone had forwarded my email to Australia where Doctor John Foote read it and contacted me. He joined our medical ministry trip to Papua New Guinea. This was such a timely miracle and answer to our prayers!

June 2015, Doctor John Foote, Larry Gardner and I ministered for 4 weeks in Papua New Guinea. 200 names were written in the Lambs Book of life. 1,803 people visited our "Free for the Poor" clinics and 161 backsliders rededicated their lives to Jesus. We donated 4 solar lighting systems to rural/bush Houses of Prayer (without electricity). We completed one water well project for an elementary school. We prayed for a lot of people!

July 2015, Jenny Hagger invited me to share my slide show presentation about our "branching out vision" in the Solomon Islands and our need of obtaining a second Tractor Well Drill Rig at "Revival SA" a city wide meeting in Adelaide, Australia on July 4. The offering from that meeting was over $30,000.00 allowing us to purchase the 49 hp tractor for the Solomon Islands. The Solomon Islands well drilling team would now be empowered to "branch out" and help the poor needing water in Munda, and other well projects!

August 2015, I hosted three Papua New Guinea Prayer Leaders in my home for 4 weeks here at IHOPKC (called "Immerse Program"). What a miracle that this visit was funded by the Papua New Guinea government! After handing over the big red and white tent to help birth the Goroko International House of Prayer, the governor, Julie Soso supplied funding to bring house of prayer leaders Pastor George, Pastor Jerry, and David Gahare from Goroko to IHOPKC for training.

September 2015, another 100% import exemption was granted for our Solomon Islands Tractor Water Well Project Shipping Container! Then Open Way Church provided funds for me to fly to Hydra Fab Manufacturing in Phoenix City, AL on September 24 to help load our Solomon Islands 20' Container! Plus, a stranger, noticing on Facebook our desire to spread the gospel to poor people in the Solomon Islands as we travel to install wells, contacted me. He blessed me with a solar-powered Jesus film projector as a free gift to evangelize the rural villages and schools without electricity!

October 2015, was my first time ever to visit Vanuatu from Oct 18 - 27. I watched God birth several new Houses of Prayer in Vanuatu. My heart was broken when I visited rural areas without electricity and got to see firsthand people in desperate need of clean water wells. Because of drought the rural people were walking 10 km to fetch drinking water from a river. Therefore I started contending for a 3rd Tractor well drilling rig to rescue the poor in Vanuatu who desperately need clean drinking water.

November 2015, I spent the whole month in the Solomon Islands. A most remarkable miracle occurred when God spoke to a filming team in Australia who purchased flights and came to Fa'arau, at their own expense, to produce a video as a gift to CW4L while I was there. God had spoken to a person, that I had never met, that it was imperative that CW4L receive funds to help the poor needing water in the Solomon Islands! He asked me if he could produce a 5-minute video to share our vision about branching out and providing water wells for villagers, without financial means, who desperately need clean drinking water.

Also in November, I shared the Jesus Film via the new solar powered projector in villages (without electricity), schools (without electricity), and prisons in the Solomon Islands. I saw many surrender their lives to Christ! I had no money, so I posted pictures of our Orphan/Visitor House which needed guttering to channel rainfall to a water tank for bathing and toilets and the money came in during that same month! I flew and spent 3 days visiting Munda, in the Western Province of the Solomon Islands, to get organized (by faith) for a 2016 water well ministry trip! I thought that if God could speak to a filming team from Australia, to come at their own expense to produce a video, to share our vision to branch out and provide water wells for villagers without the financial means who desperately need clean drinking water, then, I had better get things organized!

December 2015, finances were provided allowing me to accept Jenny Hagger's invitation to minister in Adelaide, Australia, from Dec 5-14 before flying back to Kansas City. I got to share my report on my ministry trip in Vanuatu and all that God was doing in the Solomon Islands. She then financed 4 days of rest and recreation at Kingsgate Haven on Kangaroo Island! Upon arriving back home I became seriously ill with an infection which included my doctor sending me to the emergency room here in Kansas City.

It just dawned on me, while writing this book, that I felt so helpless the first three months of 2016 as I was recovering from this illness. Our brand-new miracle 49 hp tractor well drilling rig was in storage in Honiara, Solomon Islands for those three months because I had no money to put in water wells for the poor.

During my recovery, I still maintained my 55 hours per week in the IHOPKC prayer room contending for the resources we needed to branch out to Munda in the Western Province of the Solomon Islands. Finally, I received an email asking how much money I needed to buy materials to install 10 water wells. I replied that it would require $10,000. In response, this person made a $5,000 contribution and asked me to communicate through my e-newsletter that this money was to be a challenge to the others reading my e-newsletter to sow gifts until this gift grew to $10,000, which would be used to purchase materials for our first ten wells. It took less than 30 days and our goal was achieved.

In May 2016 I received the 5-minute video from the Australian company that the Holy Spirit had put into their hearts to produce. The video was a gift to help Clean Water 4 Life secure $50,000.00 to build 25 water wells by the end of 2016. When I showed this new video to several top leaders at

IHOPKC they offered to post it on the official IHOPKC Facebook page and in one week's times it had been viewed 34,000 times, and donations began coming in.

The Australian House of Prayer in Adelaide also promoted the new Clean Water 4 Life video on their Facebook page and by sending the YouTube link in their email newsletter. Several other Australian ministries reposted this video and forwarded my e-newsletters explaining about the severe drought in the Solomon Islands, and how there was desperate need for a clean cup of water for 400,000 people living there.

Truly it is on God's heart to relieve the poor and oppressed! From June 1, 2016 through the end of the year, Clean Water 4 Life received double what I had asked for in the 5-minute Australian video. This is such an incredible testimony of God's heart. 20 water wells were sponsored from Canada, 15 water wells were sponsored from Australia, and 15 water wells were sponsored from the USA. Plus, I received $1,000 of donations from England!

The really exciting report is that Clean Water 4 Life installed 50 water wells in 2016! We had two tractors on two different Islands in two different provinces installing water wells for entire villages, schools, clinics, and churches!

What we are doing together in the Solomon Islands is truly historic! Never in the history of the Solomon Islands has a tractor well drilling rig traveled to these remote Islands without roads to install water wells for the poor and oppressed. Many remote Islands have never ever had any type of vehicle on their land and with the use of small landing crafts we show up with the good news of Jesus Christ and provide entire villages and schools much needed water wells.

In closing this chapter I'd like to share our water well program criteria. To qualify for an almost free Clean Water 4 Life water well there must be at least 50 people that will access the well. The people receiving the CW4L well must work alongside our trained team. Our team must be provided with sleeping accommodations and meals during the well installation. Upon completion of the well there must be a corporate worship service with preaching of the gospel by myself or one of the other CW4L team. We also bring our solar Jesus Film projector and show the life of Jesus during our time of installing the well. For many children, this is their first ever movie and they sit glued to the Jesus film.

With adequate funding in 2018, our two tractors are capable of sinking another 150 or more water wells. Entire villages with no electricity and without the financial means to pay for a clean drinking water well will receive the gift of a sponsored well which includes a manual hand pump. Plus they get to hear the Good News of Jesus Christ wherever we go! Over 400,000 people still need clean drinking water in the Solomon Islands!

There is no limit to the impact of our ministry as we provide both clean drinking water and – even more importantly – the living water through the preaching of the good news! Jesus said that we will by no means lose our reward for giving a cup of cold water to one of these little ones. Will you pray about partnering with Clean Water 4 Life so we can continue? To sponsor one well costs $2,500.

In 2019, I believe God would like our ministry to branch out the the nation of Vanuatu in the South Pacific. This means we need a third tractor well drilling rig and funding to sponsor water wells. I visited Vanuatu in 2015 and the severe drought has affected many on remote Islands. In one rural village I visited the villagers were walking 10 kilometers round trip to carry their drinking water from a river.

For the last two years, I have been contending in the place of prayer for a barge type landing craft to transport our tractor well drilling rig, team, and supplies from island to island.

There are 30 bible verses about the islands singing! God's vision for the islands is clear in these last days before Jesus returns. We are privileged to get this opportunity to partner with Jesus heart in the establishing of His house of prayer as mentioned in Isaiah 56:6-7.

Does Jesus weep for His children in need of a cup of cold water? Here are two Bible verses that speak His heart.

[31] *"When the Son of Man comes in His glory, and all the holy angels with Him, then He will sit on the throne of His glory.* [32] *All the nations will be gathered before Him, and He will separate them one from another, as a shepherd divides his sheep from the goats.* [33] *And He will set the sheep on His right hand, but the goats on the left.* [34] *Then the King will say to those on His right hand, 'Come, you blessed of My*

Father, inherit the kingdom prepared for you from the foundation of the world: ³⁵ *for I was hungry and you gave Me food; I was thirsty and you gave Me drink; I was a stranger and you took Me in;* ³⁶ *I was naked and you clothed Me; I was sick and you visited Me; I was in prison and you came to Me.'*

³⁷ *"Then the righteous will answer Him, saying, 'Lord, when did we see You hungry and feed You, or thirsty and give You drink?* ³⁸ *When did we see You a stranger and take You in, or naked and clothe You?* ³⁹ *Or when did we see You sick, or in prison, and come to You?'* ⁴⁰ *And the King will answer and say to them, 'Assuredly, I say to you, inasmuch as you did it to one of the least of these My brethren, you did it to Me.'*
Matthew 25:31-39

Matthew 10:42 "And **whoever gives one of these little ones** *even a cup of cold water because he is a disciple, truly, I say to you, he will by no means lose his reward.*"

Chapter 10
More Bridges

I guess one could say that my 2008 trip to Fiji was strategic. So, while in Fiji attending the 2008 Healing of the Land Conference I was introduced to 20 Church leaders from Papua New Guinea including Honorable Thompson Harokaqveh, the Member of Parliament for Goroka, the 4th largest city in Papua New Guinea. My airplane ride from Honiara, Solomon Islands stopped at the Port Vila Airport in Vanuatu where I switched to another airplane headed for Nadi, Fiji. I greeted the man seated next to me for the plane ride to Fiji. I told him my name was Rick Rupp, I was from the International House of Prayer in Kansas City and that I was headed for the Healing of The Land Conference in Fiji. He told me he was Pastor Mogia from Goroka, Papua New Guinea and that he too was traveling to the same conference along with a delegation of 23 people from PNG. As I shook hands with this new friend I had no idea God was building a bridge to Papua New Guinea, where subsequently I ministered many times and extended my Clean Water 4 life ministry.

Over the next ten days at the Healing of the Land Conference in Fiji, I met and got to know each and every one of the 23 people from Goroka, Papua New Guinea. We ate together, we had coffee breaks together, and we worshiped and prayed together. When they heard that there was a 24/7 house of prayer in Kansas City, they had many questions for me. I received two very significant invitations for future ministry in Papua New Guinea as a result of meeting this delegation at the Fiji Healing of the Land Conference.

Pastor Mogia was the Christian Chaplin at the University of Goroka, for the Goroka Technical School, and for the Nursing School in Goroka. He told me that he was also the Chaplin for all the High Schools and Elementary Schools in Goroka, including the rural schools outside the city.

Pastor Mogia said, "Papa Ricky, I invite you to bring a team of IHOPKC young people to come to Goroka to share about their involvement in the International House of Prayer in Kansas City. Our young people have never heard about day and night worship and prayer as God is doing in Kansas City. Since I am the Chaplin for all the schools I can arrange your ministry itinerary, and provide your teams transport and housing. Please come for at least a 10 day visit."

The second invitation was from Honorable Thompson Harokaqveh, the Member of Parliament for Goroka. Thompson had been motivated by witnessing the transformation happening in Fijian villages during this August 2008 trip and he was organizing the first healing of the land program for his clan's village located just outside of Goroka, for March of 2009. Wow! What an honor when Thompson invited me to come and be a part of this pilot healing of the land program in Papua New Guinea.

So, in 2009 I had the privilege of visiting Goroka, Papua New Guinea twice. First, I attended the Goroka Healing of the Land program in March of 2009. It was a life changing experience for me. It was a three-week program which included a teaching from the word of God every morning. We were fasting so our lunch time became a time of corporate praying for the community. After our prayer time, we split up into small teams of 4-6 people. We had 12 small teams and our goal was to visit every house in Thompson Harokaqveh clan's village. We would gain entrance into each home by simply asking if we could come inside and pray for the family needs. After our time of prayer with each family we then invited them to come to a community feast that was scheduled on Saturday the following week. We explained that there would be a bonfire, along with a time of repentance, at the community feast. I was praying for a move of the Holy Spirit like the event in Ephesus, described in Acts chapter 19.

Acts 19:19 ...*many of those who had practiced magic brought their books together and burned them in the sight of all. And they counted up the value of them, and it totaled fifty thousand pieces of silver.* [20] *So the word of the Lord grew mightily and prevailed.*

The Holy Spirit moved mightily and many people we had visited came on that Saturday. Some brought items used for witchcraft. Some brought drugs. Some brought cans of beer or other addictive alcoholic drinks. One by one people publicly confessed their sin and afterwards threw the drugs or witchcraft objects into the bonfire. One man brought his spear saying, "Me say sorry Jesus. Me use spear and me murder two men in da bush. Me ask You Jesus to forgive me my sin." Then he threw his spear into the fire.

I remember an older woman confessing to everyone that 30 years earlier, she had had an abortion and kept it a secret for decades. I watched Jesus set her free from the guilt and shame by confessing her secret sin. After a full afternoon of people publicly confessing all sorts of sin we ended with a worship service. It was a glorious time of high praise and worship for all that Jesus had done. Later that night everyone feasted on enough food to feed an entire village! I was seeing firsthand that God meant exactly what His Word declares in 2 Chronicles 7:14 from this experience.

Pastor Mogia was involved in the healing of the land process so God used this March trip to deepen my relationship with him. I agreed with his request to bring a team of young people from IHOPKC in September 2009, for a 10-day ministry trip to preach Jesus and call the young people in Goroka to lifestyles of prayer and fasting. I remember Mogia saying "Ricky you will stand before thousands of our youth and young adults and they need to hear that Jesus is establishing His House of Prayer in every tribe, tongue, and nation. They need to hear that in the US the young people are praying and fasting for God to send another great revival. We need our youth to embrace a lifestyle of prayer and fasting"

In September of 2009 I returned with a team of young adults from IHOPKC and Mogia was not kidding. With his help, we had a wonderful ten-day trip; we had 30 different ministry opportunities in ten days! Every morning, afternoon, and night we preached the gospel, and called people to a Joel 2 lifestyle of prayer and fasting. And yes, we truly did stand before thousands! Just at the Goroka High School, and this was one of many schools, our team stood before 1400 students of all denominations. It was so powerful to let each of these young adults share about their love for Jesus and why they had chosen to join IHOPKC.

Andy Blake from on the IHOPKC team shared that it was not okay with him that abortion was legal in America. He said that since 1973 there had been over 50 million babies aborted. Those Papua New Guinea students were stunned by Andy's testimony and amazed that he chose to spend this season of his life in prayer and fasting asking God to bring abortions in America to an end. In fact, after listening to Andy a 16-year-old boy with tears in his eyes gave me $20. He requested that I give it to someone willing to adopt one of those unwanted babies in the womb.

One of the IHOPKC young ladies shared how she had been addicted to drugs and alcohol as a teenager which then led her into sexual immorality and how Jesus had set her free. She boldly preached that Jesus was calling the youth in Goroka to walk in purity until marriage and avoid the trap of addictions.

Another young man on our team shared how at age 15 he started viewing pornography secretly online and how it grew into a full-blown addiction. He then said if Jesus was willing and able to forgive him and set him free that Jesus is capable to do the same to any student who had fallen prey to pornography.

The Holy Spirit convicted these students. We ended our time of sharing at this meeting by offering to pray for anyone that wanted prayer for any of the issues that they were struggling with.

Each person on our team was busy praying individually for the next hour as student after student came to them confessing their sin and asking Jesus for His grace and mercy to set them free from sin and shame. We had to organize the students to stand in a single file line waiting their turn for one on one prayer ministry at the Goroka High School.

Mogia also had arranged for our team to visit the Goroka Hospital to pray for the sick. We split up into two teams. Each team had a person with an acoustic guitar who could lead worship and praise songs. We were quite surprised at the conditions in this hospital because we were expecting it to be similar to US standards. We went from ward to ward, singing a couple of songs that everyone knew and many patients sang with us. After singing we shared a 10-minute sermon from the scripture about the power of Jesus at the cross to heal. We then prayed for anyone wanting us to come to their bedside for healing prayer.

We saw horrible illnesses. One young girl who was scheduled for a leg amputation uncovered and showed us her leg. She had flesh-eating bacteria which had eaten all her flesh exposing nothing but her leg bone from the ankle up to her knee. It was heart breaking for me and the others to see these suffering people. I could not believe my eyes.

A 14-year-old boy had tongue cancer. His tongue was enlarged protruding out his mouth so he could not talk or close his mouth.

Another woman opened up her hospital gown to expose the stitches from her chest to her stomach. She said the Doctor had opened her up to remove a cancerous growth but because the cancer was so advanced he simply stitched her back up telling her that only a miracle would save her life. I prayed for this woman to be healed but we saw no manifestation of healing. This lady told me that she wanted to dedicate her life to serving Jesus as an intercessor like I was doing. So, we prayed for her salvation and that God would set her on His wall as a full-time intercessor for His kingdom purposes. The team and I left the Goroka hospital not knowing if anyone was healed or would be healed.

We went straight to our housing accommodations after the hospital ministry assignment. Everyone was sick to their stomachs and asked our hosts not to prepare any food for our typical evening meal together, because they had no appetite. Everyone went into their bedrooms and I heard much weeping for the next hour as they thought about this gut-wrenching experience.

Let me fast forward now to an unusual God encounter several years later in the IHOPKC prayer room. I am praying in the IHOPKC Global Prayer Room and specifically I'm located in the Israel side room praying. (I hope you some day will come visit IHOPKC and search out for yourself what I mean by the Israel side room.)

I hear the Lord speak saying, "Rick I want you to organize medical clinics for My people in Papua New Guinea and the Solomon Islands." Frankly, I could not believe what my ears were hearing. I was so undone that I started to cry. Yes, I could feel God's heartbeat for the sick and hurting poor people but I could not understand how or why that He would ask a prayer guy with no money and no medical experience to organize medical clinics in Papua New Guinea and the Solomon Islands.

At home that evening I Skyped with a friend from Bowling Green, Ohio. I explained my God encounter and told him that I did not even know where to start with this medical clinic assignment. But my friend said, "I think I can help". He said that his brother who is a MD had just returned from a medical trip to help the poor in Africa and gave me his contact information. I emailed this MD asking him for help. His information was exactly what I needed. He told me about a Johnson & Johnson Medi Pack program that required a licensed medical doctor's signature to obtain prescription medicine and other nonprescription medicines for a fraction of the normal cost. This program was perfect! I was so excited because now I could provide a doctor with the items used in the "Free for the Poor" type medical clinics. With this new information, I contacted them. They answered all of my questions about their Medi Pack program to help the poor. I told God if He supplied the money and the doctor, yes, I could do this!

I got really excited when I found out that this program would provide me with approx. $13,000 worth of medical supplies for each $500 donation, as long as all the medicine would be given away free to poor people in need. Plus, their program required that all unused medicine be turned over to a local hospital or clinic before returning home from abroad. They also required all medicines to be carried in checked baggage. After receiving all this helpful information, I was ready and willing to pursue the organization of my first medical clinic. I started fund raising and soon had $2,000 with which I placed my order with Medi Pack for approximately $52,000 worth of medicine. The total weight was just shy of 100 pounds and everything fit into two suit cases. However, I still needed a doctor.

Some weeks later I was sharing my Islands Slide Show presentation in my living room with a group of people all involved here at IHOPKC. I showed a few photos from the Goroka Hospital experience and explained how God wanted me to organize a "Free for the Poor" medical clinic for Papua New Guinea and the Solomon Islands but that I needed a doctor. At that point, I noticed tears in one of my guest's eyes. This person asked to share something with me privately at the conclusion of my meeting. He waited until everyone had left and then said to me, "Rick you don't know this about me. But I am a retired doctor. I was crying because when I was a little boy around 5 years old my grandmother prophesied over me that one day I would be involved as a medical missionary to the poor". He continued saying, "I think I'm supposed to be your doctor for these medical clinics in Papua New Guinea and the Solomon Islands. Give me 24 hours to pray and I promise that I can give you a definite answer by tomorrow, okay?"

Wow! The next day Dr Rick Bass confirmed that he was going with me!

Our first medical missionary trip was in 2013. We spent three weeks in the Solomon Islands and then flew on to Goroka, Papua New Guinea on August 24, and stayed until September 18.

With part of the money that was contributed from my Sept 20, 2012 Call 2 All presentation I purchased and sent a Hydra Fab Trailer Well Drilling Rig and everything else needed to start a well drilling ministry to David Gahare in Papua New Guinea. I previously mentioned that I met David Gahare in 2008 at the Fiji Healing of the Land trip. Our vision was to help the poor people living in rural villages in Papua New Guinea who were in need of clean drinking water. We sent a Hydra Fab Trailer Well Drilling Rig and supplies to David prior to this trip, I was very excited that this would be our first time providing free medical ministry to the people of Papua New Guinea.

We were a four-man team flying from the Solomon Islands to Goroka, Papua New Guinea on August 24, Ricky Namo from Fa'arau well drilling team would do the well training in Goroka. Pastor Aaron Lagani would help with the well training by day and help with the preaching in the nightly services. Doctor Rick Bass would run the clinics, and I was there to help wherever needed. This was a first time experience for Ricky Namo to fly on an airplane. The four of us made a great team! I felt God's heart as I watched Ricky, a Solomon Islander, train the Papua New Guinea locals in the art of well drilling that he had just learned a year earlier.

Doctor Rick Bass set up and conducted his medical clinic with the assistance of David Gahare's wife Rebecca, a licensed RN nurse. Ricky Namo from our our Fa'arau Well Drilling Team trained David Gahare and some of his local boys in the art of installing water wells. Every night , we preached Jesus in many different churches. I had the opportunity to work with Dr Rick Bass half of each day in his clinic and then join to watch and pray as Ricky Namo conducted his well drilling training. Both were a great success. But there was much more to our trip in Papua New Guinea.

Long before this trip I had what I call an Acts 15:16 God encounter while I was praying at IHOPKC and contending for all that was in God's heart for Papua New Guinea. This Acts 15:16 encounter happened approximately one month after Dr. Rick Bass had committed to leading our medical clinics.

Acts 15:16 *"After this I will return and will rebuild the tabernacle of David, which has fallen down; I will rebuild its ruins, And I will set it up."*

God told me to buy a big tent and ship it to Goroka, Papua New Guinea as a prophetic act because He was going to birth a day and night prayer house in Goroka. By now you can probably guess my response to this request. I said "God why would you give me a ministry assignment like this? I have no money and I have no knowledge of where to buy a tent. Or even how big of a tent." Heaven was silent and I knew Jesus was smiling at me again. So, I did what I do! Once again, I scheduled a 10-day fund raising trip to Indiana, Ohio, and Michigan asking people to partner and empower me to buy and ship a big tent to Goroka, Papua New Guinea.

I did my research and got a price for a 40 ft X 80 ft tent. It would cost $8,000 and then the cost of shipping would add another $2,000. I asked the tent manufacturer for a tent big enough to hold 200 people. I had peace that this size would make a good start for the Goroka House of Prayer. But could I raise $10,000? I headed out driving first to a Church in Indiana. At the conclusion of this first Church service I was shocked and encouraged because $5,000 was contributed. God confirmed He was leading me in the tent assignment. It sure helped my weak faith when God supplied 50% of the total needed at my first church service too! So yes, my fund-raising trip achieved the $10,000 goal. I ordered and shipped the tent and I asked David Gahare to apply for a 100% exemption because I had no more money. I was hoping that the tent would arrive and be set up during our August 24 – September 15 trip to Goroka.

I remember ordering our airline tickets the first week of April 2013. Whenever possible we purchase airfare months in advance to get the cheapest possible pricing. The medical clinic dates were Aug 4 – 24 in Solomon Islands and Aug 24 – Sept 18 in Papua New Guinea.

The rest of this story is mind blowing! Something only God can orchestrate.

Back while Dr Rick Bass and I were in the Solomon Islands I received an email from David Gahare about our visit to Papua New Guinea. He tells me that the Prime Minister and other government officials were calling for a National Day of Repentance, and organizing a weekend of prayer for the entire nation of Papua New Guinea to observe on the exact weekend that our team of four was scheduled to arrive. David explained that $30,000.00 was being spent to build a big wooden stage for the Prime Minister, Members of Parliament, leaders from all the denominations, the local pastors in Goroka and Governor Julie Soso, in a big park located in the center of Goroka. David told me that they were expecting up to 5,000 people to converge on Goroka to attend this National Day of Repentance gathering.

David went on to say in his email to me that Governor Julie Soso had also had an Acts 15:16 encounter from God about birthing a prayer house in Goroka. He told me that she would publicly announce on August 26 in the park that she was putting one million kinas into a fund so that the city could build the Goroka International House of Prayer. Because Governor Julie Soso goes to David's Church he told her about my encounter and that the big tent that was coming.

So, on Dr. Rick Bass's first trip with me to Papua New Guinea, the first three days we were both invited to sit up on the big wooden stage with the Prime Minster of Papua New Guinea and 50 top leaders from the nation. We were both stunned at God's orchestration of this National Day of Repentance. I have videos of both Governor Julie

Soso and Prime Minister Peter O'Neil speaking from the stage to the thousands of people who had gathered in Goroka for the birthing of the Goroka House of prayer. We both were wowed with what we were witnessing! Here we were, sitting on the stage several chairs from Prime Minister Peter O'Neil. It just happened that we had booked our tickets back in April before this weekend event was even organized on this very weekend! I later found out from Governor Julie Soso that the literal translation for Goroka is: "The dawning of a new day." She invited Dr Rick Bass and me to her office to talk more about the meaning behind the Acts 15:16 tent.

I was asked to share publicly about the big tent I had purchased and shipped to Papua New Guinea as a prophetic act to signify that God was saying, "It is time to rebuild the tent of David and establish the Goroka House of Prayer." I'm guessing 3,000 – 5,000 people were sitting on the grass in the park as I shared with them that I was a full-time intercessor serving at a 24/7 House of Prayer in Kansas City. I told them that I lived by faith on a very low monthly budget. I wanted them to understand that this was truly a miracle. Then I explained that their tent was in storage at Port Lae, because David's attempt to obtain a 100% import exemption had been denied and I had no money to pay the duty fees. I shared with this large crowd of people that I was sorry that their red and white stripped tent was not here for them to see and be used. I told them that we needed $9,000 Kina to get their tent out of storage. I told them I felt the color red represented the power of the blood of Jesus, and the white represented Jesus taking away our sins and making us white as snow.

The next thing I knew was one of the event leaders announcing that we were taking up an offering to pay the duty fees and get Goroka their tent. I watched as ushers distributed plastic buckets along the front of the stage. The worship band and team started a song and people stood up and started walking to place their offering into the buckets. You must understand that most of the people were very poor. What a beautiful sight to behold as the people came forward with their offerings! It was a double portion offering. We needed $9,000 Kina and $18,000 Kina was given. From that offering my friend David Gahare was given the $9,000 kina he needed and approx. a week later, on Sept 7, 2013, the 40ft X 80ft red and white stripped tent was set up in Goroka!

That same day I was busy helping Dr. Rick Bass all morning and afternoon at our clinic so I did not get to witness the actual setting up of the tent. The previous day it had been handed over to the Goroka Pastor's Fraternal and I was thankful because these Pastors assured me they knew how to set up their new tent. Dr. Rick Bass and I shut down the medical clinic early that day and at 4 pm, when we arrived at location, it was already up and looked beautiful! Of course, I took lots of pictures! I don't claim to understand all this but the Holy Spirit reminded me that on Sept 7, 2012 the water started flowing at Fa'arau village. I have a photograph of the first cold cup of water at Fa'arau. This had happened exactly a year earlier. Deep within me I knew Jesus was smiling at me! The red and white tent was now set up on Sept 7 as an Acts 15:16 prophetic act symbolizing His heart for worship and prayer in the spirit of the tabernacle of David. I do know that it is by Jesus stripes that we are healed as we read in Isaiah 53:5.

Doctor Rick and I traveled together doing a total of four Free for the Poor medical clinics in the Solomon Islands and Papua New Guinea. Working together we prayed Psalm 103:3 for every person that entered our clinics. In the Solomon Islands, we had a woman paralyzed from the waist down rise up and walk after receiving prayer. In rural Papua, New Guinea, a 2-month-old infant with double pneumonia lived because the Medi Pack program had included a very expensive anti biotic specifically for infants with pneumonia, which we did not request!

Dr. Rick told every patient that visited his clinics that Jesus is the One who does the healing. He explained to his patients that all he was doing was providing them the right medicine and the Psalm 103:3 prayer. Dr. Rick loved to pray this prayer as he laid his hand on each patient. "Dear Jesus we forget not all Your benefits. It is written that You are the God who forgives all of our sins and heals all our diseases, so by the power of Your shed blood at the cross of Calvary let Your healing power flow into this one in Jesus name." Together Dr. Rick and I as a team led hundreds of people to salvation in Christ. And many who were backsliders prayed a prayer of rededication returning to following Jesus in our medical clinics.

After our August/September 2013 "Free for the Poor" medical clinics we made plans to return for another trip in 2015. We purchased our airfare on April 2, 2015. Our plan was to spend a month in Papua New Guinea May 31 - July 2. We had everything organized to provide "Free for the Poor" clinics during the day and share God's Word calling people into lifestyles of prayer every night. We made arrangements to spend one week in Mount Hagen, one week in Goroka, one week in Madang, and the last week at Mount Michael. Then tragedy struck when Dr Rick Bass was killed while riding his motorcycle on May 4, 2015 in Texas.

Now what? How do you do a medical clinic without a doctor? It took me several days to get over the shock and it seemed like God was saying to continue as planned and go on this trip in honor of Dr. Rick Bass. As mentioned earlier, On May 7, I sent out an email asking people to join me in praying for a doctor to work in Dr. Rick's place for our June 1 – July 1 trip to Papua New Guinea.

Are you ready for another miracle?

My dear friend Jenny Hagger in Adelaide, Australia forwarded my email to everyone on her ministry email list connected with the Australian House of Prayer. She asked everyone to pray for a doctor. On May 11th, just 20 days prior of our trip I received an email from Dr. John Foote a 79-year-old retired doctor living in Adelaide, Australia. Dr. John said that he wanted to talk to me about replacing Dr.

Rick Bass for our Papua New Guinea trip. His wife, Lorraine, had received Jenny Hagger's email and said, "John come over here and read this email, because you could do this." In fact, Dr. John, had been praying for an opportunity to return to Papua New Guinea where he had served in a hospital for many years. After our skype call Dr. John asked me to email him all of the flight information. He explained to me that if he was able to book all the exact same flights and if he could get his expired passport renewed in time, he would like to be my replacement doctor. Someone once told me that if it is God's vision, He will release all the provision! The very next day I received an email confirmation that Dr. John had successfully booked on all the same flights and on May 30th he emailed that his passport and visa had also come through just in time for his May 31 flight to Brisbane. We met each other for the first time in Brisbane Airport and flew off together for a wonderful ministry trip in Papua New Guinea! However, the June 2015 clinic was my last "Free for the Poor" medical clinic, I am believing God to raise up several doctors so we can resume our clinics again in 2017.

Chapter 11
Rick Bass

Back in 2012, I was sharing my Solomon Islands/Papua New Guinea slide show presentation in my living room with a group of people from the International House of Prayer in Kansas City, Missouri. It was quite normal for me to invite 10 -15 people over to my home for an evening of showing my pictures and telling lots of God stories from my numerous trips to Goroka, Papua New Guinea and Fa'arau, Solomon Islands.

However, that particular night, there was this guy named Rick Bass in attendance. I knew that Rick was a core leader for one of the IHOPKC internships and that he was part of our full-time staff at IHOPKC, but that was about it. Part of my slide show included sharing photos of sick people in the Goroka Hospital in Papua New Guinea. As I was sharing about the conditions at the Goroka Hospital, I noticed tears in Rick Bass' eyes.

During my Islands Presentation, I shared how God had spoken to me that on my next trip we would be doing medical clinics for the poor in both the Solomon Islands and Papua New Guinea. I explained that God had supplied $2,000 for the purchase of $50,000 worth of medical products through a program offered by Johnson & Johnson called MAP. I explained that MAP requires a licensed doctor and this program is offered for third world countries, as long as "Free for the Poor" medical clinics are offered.

And, as mentioned earlier, it was then that Dr. Rick joined me and we had quite a journey together! We prayed together and watched God release provision for medical supplies, well drilling equipment, musical instruments, Bibles, and even an Orphan/Visitors House in Fa'arau, Solomon Islands!

It's important for you to know that Rick Bass arrived at Fa'arau (Trip #1) on Aug 7, 2013, and there were some funny looks on his face as we took the boat ride from Honiara to Auki, which is the port city on the Island of Malaita, where God birthed a 24/7 House of Prayer in a jungle village without electricity or running water. These jobless people are very poor by worldly standards, but very rich in their worship, prayer, and praise to God!

I'll never forget the look on Dr. Rick's face when we all piled into the back of a 3-ton flatbed truck transporting us from Auki to Fa'arau on a very bumpy gravel road. During the 12-kilometer ride, it poured down rain and Rick got drenched. We all laughed and said welcome to the Solomon Islands! Many things impacted Rick, but I'll mention the two main things that kept Rick wanting to return with me on future ministry trips:

1. The presence of God during the worship and prayer at Fa'arau House of Prayer. Rick loved it there! I don't recall how many times he told me that he was sure he heard angels singing or joining with the congregational singing.
2. Rick also recognized that there was something special in this village. Rick told me from day one that he felt as if he was at home with family.

Rick loved the village bush hut that was built and provided for his medical clinic at Fa'arau. Over the two weeks, 1300 poor and needy people were diagnosed and treated, and each person received individual prayer. It was amazing for me to watch

Rick in his element. He patiently listened to each person explaining their ailment. The climate was very hot and humid, with no fan or air conditioning, yet he never complained. The compassion and care the people received was truly remarkable. There was a special grace on Dr. Rick that allowed him to see an average of 80 patients per day!

From Solomon Islands, we flew on together to Goroka, Papua New Guinea on Aug 24th, for a ministry trip. In Goroka, Dr. Rick did medical clinics. He also helped me with nightly preaching. He even got involved a few days in helping Ricky Namo with the installation of a water well for David Gahare.

One of the highlights of the Papua New Guinea medical clinics trip was setting up his clinic in a poor rural village approx. 45 minutes outside of Goroka. It was an outdoor clinic in the bush and the people living there were able to provide us a table, but nobody had any chairs. So, they brought Dr Rick an old empty 40-gallon drum which he used as his chair. We called it the "Rick Bass Bush Barrel Clinic".

At this clinic, a mother brought her infant child, who was dying of double pneumonia. Rick smiled and whispered in my ear that the Johnson & Johnson MAP program had included a very expensive antibiotic which was for infants with pneumonia! That baby lived and only God knows if perhaps that child will grow up to be another Billy Graham. My point is that God had supplied exactly what we needed and we marveled. And if God had not sent us to *that* village on *that* day to *that* infant, according to Dr. Rick, he never would have lived. We both agreed that sick infant baby must have a special calling on his life.

Well, I'll wrap up this tribute by saying that we were both looking forward to doing another month-long clinic in Papua New Guinea together again in 2015 from May 31 - July 2, plus spending our final weekend with our friends at the Australian House of Prayer in Adelaide, Australia before flying back to Kansas City. In fact, Dr. Rick was looking forward to also returning to the Solomon Islands. Dr. Rick had asked me to organize a 6 week visit back to the Solomon Islands for us to do "Free for the Poor" clinics again in October & November 2015, six months after his tragic accident.

When something so unexpected, like the death of a dear friend, happens, what is one to do? At this point, I'm simply praying for Rick's wife, Deborah and all their family. I say, "Yes and amen" to God's promises even when I don't understand. I acknowledge that God's ways are higher. I know that Dr. Rick would want me to continue with our medical clinics to the poor. So, I'm expecting God will supply another Doctor quickly. I believe that Rick's death will be a seed in the ground for the expansion of the work in the South Pacific. Nothing will hinder the plans of the Lord.

In honor of my friend Dr. Rick Bass (August 5, 1951 – May 4, 2015)

Praise report: just prior to the publishing of this book, I found out that our "Free For The Poor" medical clinics will resume soon. On July 29, 2017 I married Dr Grace Lea Kim who is eager to join me. Plus another doctor from Emporia, Kansas is committed to start going with us! Praise God!

Epilogue

What do Intercessory Missionaries do in Prayer Rooms?

1. We minister to God by declaring His worth unceasingly, reflecting the way He receives worship continually in heaven (Matthew 6:10). We magnify the supremacy of Jesus, spreading His fame by declaring His worth, beauty, and riches, calling others to love and obey Him and give their allegiance to Him. Millions of people across the nations join the choirs of heaven by ministering to God in this way. He is worthy.

2. We labor in intercession to release God's power to win the lost, revive the Church, and impact society as we do works of justice and compassion.

3. We grow in intimacy with God by personally encountering Him through His Indwelling Spirit, receiving greater grace to love, obey, and

partner with Him, as we are fascinated by who He is.

4. We grow in the understanding of God's Word, gaining insight into His will, ways, and salvation and learning about the unique dynamics of His end-time plan to transition the earth to the age to come. We serve others in an important way by taking the time and effort to grow deeper in understanding the Word, that we may help others understand God's heart and will for this hour of history.

What's Happening In The Prayer Movement Today?

The Holy Spirit has raised up thousands of new prayer ministries in the last ten to twenty years. In 1984, the number of 24/7 houses of prayer in the world was fewer than 25. Today, there are over 10,000—most of that growth has been in the last ten years. They are springing up all over the globe at a staggering rate. Such momentum in prayer cannot be attributed to human ingenuity, but rather to the sovereign work of the Holy Spirit.

The significant increase of new 24/7 prayer ministries and of large prayer events in stadiums is a prophetic sign of the times—a sign of the approaching day of the Lord's return. In cities around the world, new 24/7 prayer ministries are being established. From Kiev, Bogota, and Jerusalem to New Zealand, Cairo, Cape Town, and Hong Kong, men and women are responding to the Spirit's leadership in this.

Despite the pressures and inherent dangers, we see 24/7 prayer centers coming forth in the Muslim world, in nations like Egypt, Turkey, Syria, Indonesia, and Lebanon.

God's desire to be worshiped on earth as He is in heaven has not changed. I believe that some of the principles expressed in the order of worship that God commanded David to embrace are timeless, such as establishing the full-time occupation of singers and musicians in God's house.

Not everyone is called to be an intercessory missionary. The greatest ministry is to do the will of God. In other words, the greatest ministry you can have is the one to which God called you. If He called you to serve in the marketplace or in your home, don't despise your calling by imitating the ministry of another. We must embrace our own individual calling, because that it is the highest calling for us.

The Holy Spirit has not emphasized the calling to night-and-day worship and prayer worldwide throughout church history, but He is now calling many ministries to embrace it. I do not believe that it is God's will for every local church or ministry to host 24/7 worship in their building, but rather I believe that He plans to establish it in each city or region of the earth. This can happen if many local churches partner together in the work of night-and-day prayer. The practical application will differ in each culture, in each city, and in each nation.

Many are asking the Lord to establish 24/7 prayer with worship in every tribe and tongue before the Lord returns—not in one building, but in every region of the earth, uniting many ministries together to accomplish the work. Imagine a mission's movement that reaches every tribe and tongue—the gospel being preached in every language—deeply connected to 24/7 prayer with worship.

Will you join me in asking the Lord to establish one million full-time intercessory missionaries before the Lord returns, whether they are singers, musicians, sound technicians, intercessors, or gatekeepers maintaining the systems that support these prayer ministries? For some of you, this is your calling—your personal story is deeply linked to God's plan related to the end-time prayer movement. What a glorious privilege!

Questions I'm often asked:

On occasion people ask me about my journey of quitting my job in Topeka, Kansas and by faith starting my time of serving at IHOPKC. They ask what motivated me to spend long hours in prayer and what motivated me to switch to the night watch for so many years. The truth is simply that I was in pain and God spoke audibly that, likewise, His heart was in pain and my Pastor confirmed the change to the night watch. I was very fortunate to have wise counsel from my Pastor in Topeka, Kansas.

I love Psalm 51:17 *"The sacrifices of God are a broken spirit; **a broken and contrite heart**, O God, you will not despise."*

Now look at Isaiah 57:15 *"For thus says the One who is high and lifted up, who inhabits eternity, whose name is Holy: 'I dwell in the high and holy place, and also with him who is of a contrite and lowly spirit, to revive the spirit of the lowly, and to revive the heart of the contrite.'"*

Truthfully, I was in so much pain from the rejection of my divorce. The shame I walked in was paralyzing. In May of 2001 when I arrived and joined IHOPKC as a full-time intercessor my view of God was wrong. I thought God was mad. That He had a big stick and I was going to get what I deserved. I found it very difficult to pray to a God that was upset with me. I now realize just how wrong my thinking was about God's love and mercy. I also realize that to break these strongholds in the mind that I needed the power of God's Word to wash over me.

Now I marvel at the wisdom of spending long hours in loving meditation in God's Word and being in a chair in a 24/7 prayer room together with other broken people. My broken heart mended slowly as I listened to prophetic singers sing God's Word sometimes 12 or more hours per day. My favorite chorus that the IHOPKC singers would sing is from Psalm 145:8-9.

*[8] The L*ORD *is gracious and full of compassion, Slow to anger and great in mercy. [9] The L*ORD *is good to all, And His tender mercies are over all His works.*

The prophetic singers would make choruses from verses like these and sing them over and over. Than I would join in the chorus and start singing with them. I would go home singing these prophetic choruses as I drove my car. In fact, I sing a lot now. My roommates hear me singing as I do cleaning and other activities around my house.

Psalm 103:8-9

*The L*ORD *is merciful and gracious, Slow to anger, and abounding in mercy. [9] He will not always strive with us, Nor will He keep His anger forever. [10] He has not dealt with us according to our sins, Nor punished us according to our iniquities. [11] For as the heavens are high above the earth, So great is His mercy toward those who fear Him; [12] As far as the east is from the west, So far has He removed our transgressions from us. [13] As a father pities his children, So the L*ORD *pities those who fear Him. [14] For He knows our frame; He remembers that we are dust.*

My time here at IHOPKC has helped give me revelation of what Ephesians 5:18-20 means: *"And do not be drunk with wine, in which is dissipation; but be filled with the Spirit, [19] speaking to one another in psalms and hymns and spiritual songs, singing and making melody in your heart to the Lord, [20] giving thanks always for all things to God the Father in the name of our Lord Jesus Christ."*

Also, Colossians 3:16, *"Let the word of Christ dwell in you richly in all wisdom, teaching and admonishing one another in psalms and hymns and spiritual songs, singing with grace in your hearts to the Lord."*

IHOPKC has been my personal singing seminary. A prayer room where singers and musicians sing psalms and hymns and spiritual songs continually! I have no regrets for the long hours that I have spent soaking in the IHOPKC prayer room. I have no regrets for living a fasted lifestyle for the past 16 years. Shutting down the entertainment was part of the healing process. If you would have told me that Rick Rupp was only to visit the movie theater 3 times in fifteen years, or that he would not watch any TV including sports for fifteen years, or that he would not use a telephone for 15 years, truthfully, I would have laughed at the idea. But God gently was offering me an invitation into His heart.

During this time, my heart was being revived as Isaiah 57:15 says: *"to revive the spirit of the lowly, and to revive the heart of the contrite."* I was privileged to sit under some of the best Bible teaching here at IHOPKC and my views changed on how God thinks and feels about me. This was another huge factor for reviving my broken heart. Check out MikeBickle.org for yourself.

During this season at IHOPKC God gave me a new identity which is: "I am in love with God and God's in love with me. This is who I am and who I will be. So, Rick Rupp, just get over it!"

I now pray to a God who likes me! I'm His favorite! I pray positive prayers from God's Word. My weak little prayers really matter. My highest calling is to fellowship (talk) with Jesus! He set me as a watchman to stand in the gap and pray until He makes Jerusalem a praise in the earth. I schedule my prayer time and consider my prayer time a priority. I use a prayer list to help me stay focused. God has ambushed my heart for the poor in the South Pacific Islands.

I'll conclude with one more cool God story. I was talking to God about a Bible verse to celebrate our IHOPKC ten-year anniversary on May 7, 2009. I was looking at New Testament verses in chapter 5 and verse 7 representing 5/7/2009. I finally found the perfect verse in 2 Corinthians 5:7 *"For we walk by faith, not by sight."* As I sat in my chair in the IHOPKC prayer room I said "God this is a perfect anniversary verse for IHOPKC!" God then said "Rick there is another anniversary this month. Look further down the page and read 2 Corinthians 5:17. It says, *"Therefore, if anyone is in Christ, he is a new creation; old things have passed away; behold, all things have become new."*

I said "God I don't get what anniversary this scripture relates to in Your heart." God smiled and said, "Rick, it was May 17, 2001 when you arrived here at IHOPKC to begin your journey."

Father of Glory it's me again. Your favorite! The one You enjoy praying for everyone who takes time to read Walk With God. Dear God pour out the Spirit of wisdom and revelation in the knowledge of who You are. Speaking to everyone who reads this book to know the hope of Your calling. Inspire every person to pray these three golden nuggets found in the Book of Ephesians in Jesus name. Amen

For more information and additional testimonies about the work in the Solomon Islands and Papua New Guinea, go to CleanWater4Life.com and CleanWater4Life.com.au.

For information about how Rick can serve you by praying for you and/or your business, go to rickrupp.com/partners.

Appendix

Teachings by Mike Bickle

List of prayers in the Bible:

mikebickle.org.edgesuite.net/MikeBickleVOD/2008/K
ey_Apostolic_Prayers_and_Intercessory_Promises.pdf

How to Prayer-Read the Word:

mikebickle.org.edgesuite.net/MikeBickleVOD/2015/2
0150403_How_to_Pray-Read_the_Word.pdf

Ten Prayers to Strengthen Our Inner Man:

mikebickle.org.edgesuite.net/MikeBickleVOD/2009/2
0090201_Ten_Prayers_to_Strengthen_Our_Inner_Ma
n_F-E-L-L-O-W-S-H-I-P_PSM04.pdf

The Spirit of the Tabernacle of David:

mikebickle.org.edgesuite.net/MikeBickleVOD/2013/2
0130604_%20The_Spirit_of_the_Tabernacle_of_Davi
d.pdf

The Call to be a Full-Time Intercessory Missionary*[3]:

mikebickle.org.edgesuite.net/MikeBickleVOD/2013/2
0131217_The_Call_to_be_an_Intercessory_Missionary
.pdf

---

[3] Permission granted.

Made in the USA
Lexington, KY
22 October 2017